'THE NAVVIES'

by

Norman L. Middlemiss

SHIELD PUBLICATIONS LTD

NEWCASTLE-upon-TYNE

GREAT BRITAIN

ISBN 1 871128 17 X

British Library Cataloguing in Publication Data

A Catalogue Record is available from the British Library

Published by :- SHIELD PUBLICATIONS LTD
P.O. BOX 5
LOW FELL
GATESHEAD.
TYNE & WEAR.
ENGLAND
NE9 7YS.

Printed by :- SMITH SETTLE LTD
Ilkley Road,
OTLEY.
W. YORKS. LS21 3JP.

CONTENTS

Frontispiece: **CRESTED EAGLE of 1925 and GOLDEN EAGLE of 1909**
racing down to Margate. (G.S.N.C. Painting)

INTRODUCTION

The General Steam Navigation Co. Ltd was the first shipping company to own sea-going steamers when trading started in 1821, with its incorporation following three years later in 1824. The recently defunct Clyde Shipping Co. Ltd could claim to be older, starting in 1815 but only with river craft between Glasgow and Port Glasgow. Most people will remember the 'Navvies' - a term applied not only to the ships but also to the men of the company - operating in the short-sea trades to Germany, Holland, Belgium, North French ports, Bordeaux and to the Mediterranean. What is not commonly known is that the company operated deep-sea liner services to West Africa, and on charter to South and North American ports during a seven year period of 1894 to 1901, fulfilling its original charter of 1824 :-

'to undertake world-wide trading with India, North and South America, Portugal, Spain, France, Holland, Germany and Russia'

The company had established its Mediterranean services in 1882 to the west coast of Italy and Sicily, which was to be the basis of its services to that region for over eighty years. Ports served included :-

Malaga and Valencia in Spain
Bastia in Corsica
Algiers and Oran in North Africa
Genoa, Catania, Civitavecchia, Livorno, Marsala, Messina, Naples, Palermo, Pozzuoli, Savona, Spezia, Syracuse in Italy
Patras and Piraeus in Greece
Izmir and Istanbul in Turkey
Black Sea ports

The company fleet was huge in numbers, and if one includes its four shipowning subsidiaries of Moss - Hutchison Line, Great Yarmouth Shipping Co. Ltd, Grand Union Shipping Co. Ltd and the New Medway Steam Packet Co. Ltd the grand total of ships is four hundred. However half of the General Steam fleet started their careers with the company before 1880, and this is the main reason why the fleet has never been documented before. Little of the early company records survive, and Lloyd's Registers do not hold the relevant information of their subsequent careers. Thus a limitation has to be placed on the amount of information of the fates of the early ships, for the simple fact that it does not exist. Certainly, the research into the fleet has been the most difficult of over one hundred British shipping companies that the author has undertaken. However, with this proviso, the fleet's history is fascinating, and extends from the beginning of the 19th century to the approach of a new millennium in the 21st century - a period of almost two hundred years. The original centenary company history published in 1924 was entitled 'One Hundred Years of Sea Trading' - an alternative title to this volume could be 'Two Hundred Years of Sea Trading' !

I am indebted particularly to Capt. Gordon Renshawe for his deep knowledge of the company and writing his recollections of summer excursions on *Golden Eagle* in 1949, published in an appendix. The company were pioneers in this field, their involvement in the summer excursion trades lasting from 1821 to 1966. The Thames and near Channel excursion trades were immensely popular during all of this time, probably more so than on the Clyde, the Bristol Channel, and South Coast. The company took over the excursion fleet of the New Medway Steam Packet Co. Ltd in 1936, and their combined fleets rank in size along with any of the Clyde companies, or P. & A. Campbell's White Funnel Steamers, or Souhampton's Red Funnel Steamers, or Cosen's steamers from Bournemouth and Weymouth.

I would also like to thank Michael Payne and John Hill for their research into the early company ships - a difficult task ! Also many thanks to Barbara Jones and Anne Cowne for their usual tireless and efficient service at Lloyd's Register of Shipping. The bibliography consulted includes :-

G.S.N.C. 'Newsletter' - the Company house magazine - 1941/71
'One Hundred Years of Sea Trading' by L. Cope Cornford published by the company in 1924.
'Semper Fidelis' - Saga of the 'Navvies' by H. E. Hancock published by the company in 1949.
'Steamers of the Thames & Medway' and 'Cross Channel and Coastal Paddle Steamers' both by Frank Burtt.
'History of the Port of London' by Sir J. G. Broodbank

Norman L. Middlemiss

Newcastle-upon-Tyne

January, 1999

WOODEN PADDLERS

The Thames river scene in 1800 was one in which the sailing ship reigned supreme, with East Indiamen, Cape Horners and other deep-sea craft thronging the fairway. A multitude of masts and rigging was visible along the wharves near the twin white domes of Greenwich or at the buoys in the river. Droves of North East collier brigs were moored in fours and sixes at the river tiers and were discharged by small craft such as the lighters owned by William Cory, who had started in business some fifteen years earlier. The lighters were filled with black diamonds by the coal whippers using stout baskets to transfer the coal from the holds of the brigs, and then drifted upstream with the tide to the City wharves aided by the long oars or sweeps of the lightermen. However this tranquil form of transport was soon to be transformed and swept aside by the new age of steam power being developed at that time on the Clyde.

James Watt (1736 - 1819), who began his career as a laboratory technician at Glasgow University, had perfected the first rotative steam engine by 1781, and it was then adapted for maritime use by fellow Glaswegian William Symington (1763 - 1831). His steam engine with two vertical cylinders drove two paddles mounted one behind the other between the twin hulls of a catamaran-type vessel. This 25 feet long steamboat was financed by Patrick Miller, an Edinburgh banker and landowner, and made its maiden voyage, reaching a speed of 5 knots, on Dalswinton Loch near Dumfries in October,1788. Among the passengers was the poet Robert Burns, and Symington went on to construct a second similar craft. This was five years after the Marquis Jouffroy d'Abbans had built the world's first steamboat on the river Saone in Eastern France. Symington was then commissioned to design a steam tug of 56 feet length driven by a stern paddle wheel by Lord Dundas, Chairman of the Forth & Clyde Canal Company. This he constructed in 1801 with a small single-cylinder double-acting engine of 10 nominal horse power, and thus *Charlotte Dundas* became the first commercial steamship in the world when she towed two laden 70-ton barges for six hours along 19.5 miles of the Canal against a head wind. The boiler and engine were abreast of each other with the engine on the port side connected to the wheel by a rod and crank as used in later engines. However her career on the Canal was relatively short as the directors of the company considered that the slight damage to the banks of the canal from her wash was greater than her advantages over the conventional horse-drawn method.

Glasgow shipowners however quickly saw the commercial advantages to be gained from such craft moving goods down the Clyde estuary by towing lighters, and by 1805 similar craft were in use between Glasgow and Greenock. The American inventor Robert Fulton operated the world's first successful regular passenger steamboat service on the Hudson river in 1807 using the pioneer steamboat *Clermont*. However the Clyde became the breeding ground of experimental steamship operation as it is favoured by relatively sheltered estuarial weather and sea conditions. By 1815 some eighteen steamers were in operation on the Clyde with another ten in use at the eastern end of the Forth & Clyde Canal on the Firth of Forth and on the Tay. At Port Glasgow the 43 feet long paddle steamer *Comet* was launched in 1812 from the yard of John Wood & Company, which later was merged into the much bigger Lithgows yard. She carried passengers down the Clyde from Glasgow to Greenock making three trips weekly in each direction and thus has her place in history as the first steamship to carry paying customers in Europe. She was the brainchild of Henry Bell, a hotel proprietor at Helensburgh, and was later used on the Firth of Forth, and after lengthening between Glasgow and Fort William. She was wrecked at Craignish Point on 13th December,1820 on one such voyage. She was the forerunner of literally hundreds of Clyde-built passenger carrying steam paddle vessels, and a replica of her, built 150 years later, is preserved in Port Glasgow shopping centre on the other side of the road from the now silent Lithgow yard.

The first paddle steamer to carry passengers on the Thames was the *Richmond*, which plied between London and Richmond in 1814. In the same year the Clyde paddler *Marjorie* paddled her way down the length of the Irish Sea and along the South Coast to work on the Thames, and two years later became the first steamship to cross the English Channel. Later in 1816 the paddle steamer *Majestic* was the first to operate out of Dover when she ran a single excursion for 200 passengers to Calais, and she also operated from Brighton to Le Havre in 1817. In 1815 the Clyde paddler *Elizabeth* reached the Mersey, and began the first steamer operation between Liverpool and Runcorn. The first paddler to operate in Belfast Lough was *Greenock* of 98 tons in 1816 on arrival from the Clyde and she spent the summer on excursions before heading south for the Thames. The first regular Glasgow/Belfast services began in June, 1818 with the paddler *Rob Roy*, which was sold to French owners in 1820 to begin the first regular Dover/Calais services as *Henri Quatre*. James Little of Greenock started a regular passenger steamship service between Greenock and Liverpool in 1819 with calls at Douglas, Isle of Man. He increased the number of ships to three in 1820 with the *Majestic* and *City of Glasgow* making the Mersey from the Clyde in 25 hours on this summer-only service. The vigorous St. George's Steam Packet Co. Ltd of Liverpool began services between Liverpool and Glasgow with the celebrated pioneer paddle steamer *St. George* in 1821, and this pioneering liner company was soon involved in other Irish Sea and North Sea services, as well as with the pioneer crossing of the Atlantic on *Sirius* in 1838.

Thus in 1817 the Thames could muster some five paddle-driven steamboats in use, and this prompted two London businessmen, William John Hall and Thomas Brockelbank, to seek partners for the purpose of founding a shipping company. William John Hall operated vessels between London and Hull; and Thomas Brockelbank was a Greenwich timber merchant who built the wooden paddle steamer *Eagle* in his own yard at Deptford in 1820. The latter vessel proved very successful in carrying excursion passengers to Margate and Ramsgate, and persuaded other businessmen running packets on the same route to join the new company, which made a preliminary start in 1821. However, oppostion to the steamship from the entrenched sailing ship fraternity meant that men with vision and money for such a venture were hard to find, and it was not until 11th June, 1824 that a motion voting for the incorporation of the company took place at the Custom House Quay belonging to William John Hall. The intention was to turn an existing company owned by Thomas Brockelbank, into a joint stock company to be called the **General Steam Navigation Co. Ltd**. The company was to have a capital of £2M to be divided into shares of £100 each of which only 10% was to be called upon from each shareholder in four equal instalments of £2 ten shillings. The following 18 directors were elected to the company on 27th July, 1824 :-

William John Hall	Thomas Brockelbank
William J. Jolliffe	Hylton Jolliffe M.P.
Matthias Attwood M.P.	Sir Edward Banks
William Bell	John Jones
Thomas S. Benson	Lt. Col. Landmann
James H. Deacon	Henry Mylius

W. John de Buck
William C. Damant
Thomas Hamlet
Charles Pearson jnr.
Michael Shepley
John Wilkin

Hylton Jolliffe M.P. was the first Chairman from 1824 - 1828

Trustees were Matthias P. Lucas, William Thompson M.P., John P. Robinson
Auditors were Capt. James Duberley, James Lett, Jacob G. Wrench
Bankers were Spooner, Attwoods & Company
Solicitors were Tilson & Preston

The company was affectionately known as the **'Navvies'** and its prospectus stated that it was formed to undertake world-wide trading with India, North & South America, Portugal, Spain, France, Holland and Russia. However the company confined nearly all of its subsequent trading to the home trade between the ports of Hamburg and Gibraltar, and from 1882 entered Mediterranean trading to Italy. The fortunes of other companies that entered the deep-sea trades were observed to see if they fared much better, and deep-sea liner services to West Africa and on charter to North and South America were later undertaken. The prospectus did however assure future shareholders that 'the national benefits arising from the power of steam are so universally acknowledged that it appears unnecessary to dwell upon its many advantages. Ships are enabled to enter and quit harbour regardless of winds or tides, and it affords the most flattering prospects of connecting the remotest parts of the world by a more safe and rapid communication'.

The first offices of the company were established at 24 Crutched Friars in October, 1824, and the first two steam packets in the fleet were *Lord Melville* (Capt. Middleton) and *Earl of Liverpool* (Capt. Peake). The latter ran to Ostend with the chartered *Mountaineer* (Capt. Mate) in 16 hours every Wednesday and Saturday, while the former ran with *Attwood* (Capt. Stranack) to Calais in 12 hours every Monday, Wednesday, Thursday and Saturday from London. Orders for three new paddle steamers, each of 240 tons, were placed for operation between Brighton/Dieppe, London/Yarmouth, and London to Rotterdam. By the end of 1824 the company owned 15 steamships, increasing to twenty steamers a year later, with 28 operating in 1826. A handbill of 1826 shows that *Harlequin* (Capt. Corbin), *City of London* (Capt. Martin), *Columbine* (Capt. Grant) and *Royal Sovereign* (Capt. Major) were running from London to Margate every morning and to Ramsgate every Wednesday and Saturday mornings.

Weekly services were also started to Rotterdam with *Belfast* (Capt. Roberts) in 26 hours, and to Hamburg with *Sir Edward Banks* (Capt. Howlett) and *Hylton Jolliffe* (Capt. Mowll) in 54 hours, and to Lisbon and Gibraltar with *George IV* (Capt. Black) and *Duke of York* (Capt. Mowle) - calling at Brighton, Portsmouth, Vigo and Oporto - while another cross-Channel connection ran from Portsmouth to Havre. The chartered *Rapid* was working the London to Boulogne route twice a week, however the paddle steamers were not fast enough to run day excursions to France from either London, Brighton or Portsmouth, and this had to wait until later when paddle steamer speeds had surpassed 18 knots. It is interesting to note that passenger's baggage, horses and carriages were loaded via wide gangways at this time, and that 'elegant state cabins' were available on board for ladies and their female attendants. Children under the age of 12 years and servants travelled free or at much reduced rates.

EAGLE of 1820 was a great success running to Margate under Capt. Martin (G.S.N.C.)

MARGATE

The company contributed greatly to the development of Margate as a resort in the 1820s, the resort previously had a poor reputation for smuggling and wrecking with its many caves used to store contraband. Shortly after the introduction of *Eagle* in 1820 the 'Sunday Times' recorded its approval of pioneer efforts to begin passenger services down the Thames to Margate in the following words :-

'The Public are highly indebted to the General Steam Navigation Company for the public spirit they have so laudably exhibited in applying the great discovery of Steam Navigation to the purposes of trade, warfare, quick communication, and of amusement. They recently accomplished a journey which a few years back would have been considered incredible and impracticable, that of going to Margate and back in one day. This great and singular undertaking completely succeeded. The performance of the voyage (nearly 160 miles) in a little more than 15 hours really constitutes an era in the history of navigation'.

Margate as a resort was very popular with Victorian Londoners, and the arrival of the 'Saturday boat', which brought Londoners down for the weekend, was a great social event. Margate Pier was built to replace a wooden jetty in the late Victorian period, and the second *Eagle* of 1853 with a service speed of 14.25 knots ran down to Margate and Ramsgate and stayed there for the night, returning on the following day. The third *Eagle* of 1898 had a service speed of just over 18 knots and could reach Margate direct in a little over four hours, and she continued her very popular day trips until 26th August,1928. The twin-funnelled *Royal Daffodil* of 1939 is shown departing below from Margate Pier on one of her daily summer excursions.

At the first Annual General Meering Hylton Jolliffe as Chairman described the extraordinary difficulties encountered by the company during its first year of trading. These had to do with opposition from sailing ship owners, the dislike of steamers by seafarers, and the profound resentment of them by watermen, lightermen and bargemen. The watermen had their business of conveying passengers up and down the Thames stolen by the steamers, and the lightermen were aggrieved because the wash of the steamers caused their boats to range against each other and sink. The disturbance of the water by the steamers prevented the bargemen from taking full cargoes for fear of capsize, and washed away the soft sand of the river bottom so that vessels resting on the bottom by the falling tide were set down on hard rock damaging their hulls. The watermen and lightermen waged war on the steamers by pulling their boats right across the path of the steamers, and then waited on their oars. When they were cut down, as they frequently were, they accused the steamship companies of deliberately running them down and sought recompense.

The political system of the time also greatly contributed to the difficulties, with much turbulence by the people to extend the basic election by ballot - votes for Catholics was conceded in 1829 - and in 1832 Grey's Reform Bill introduced a more balanced but still limited representation of the population that favoured rich landowners. The movement of some of the population from agricultural working to industrial work in overcrowded towns was another source of trouble as food then became scarce and unemployment high as people fought for work in the towns. The repeal of laws in 1824 preventing the formation of trade unions helped, as did the repeal of the Navigation Acts which greatly helped trade by allowing overseas ships full access to British ports and by reciprocity British ships were allowed full access to the ports of foreign nations. Under the circumstances the first year's dividend of 16%, was very good, and even 10% in the following year was up to expectations.

The famous Brighton Chain pier had opened in 1823, and within a few years the chartered *Rapid* (Capt. Jennings) was transferred to a Brighton to Dieppe service, and later ran on Newhaven to Dieppe services. *Eclipse* began a twice-weekly sailing from Newhaven to Dieppe in June,1825, however Brighton pier was more popular for the Dieppe run with *Eclipse* (Capt. Cheeseman) and *Talbot* (Capt. Norwood) making the passage in 8 hours in conjunction with the Brighton Steam Packet Company's *Quentin Durward* each weekday excepting weekends. The Brighton Chain pier was erected for the new cross-Channel packets with all tides boarding but was limited in rough weather and by the ships having to detour to Shoreham for servicing. In 1842 the company began to operate a steamer between Havre and Shoreham, and in October,1843 agreed to co-ordinate Shoreham/Dieppe services with the London, Brighton & South Coast Railway Company, whose line had just reached Brighton. In April,1844 the company provided two steamers, *Fame* and *Magnet*, for a service four days/week between Shoreham and Dieppe in addition to *Menai* between Shoreham and Havre. In 1849 the company provided a variety of craft from their extensive fleet temporarily for a railway company-operated Newhaven - Dieppe service, as railway companies were not permitted to own ships until 1863. Brighton Chain pier was the first British seaside pier, and had three pairs of sturdy twin iron towers linking the landing stage with the shore, with the wooden decking supported by chains that were embedded some 54 feet into the cliff. The pier gave 73 years of service before being wrecked in a heavy gale blowing up suddenly from the south-east during the night of 4th December,1896.

The excursions to Margate and Ramsgate were proving extremely popular, and for several years the company and its competitors, e.g. the Margate Steam Packet Company (purchased 1836), were carrying one million passengers/annum and sometimes well in excess of that figure. The company in 1826 established a trade in live cattle from the Continent to London, which continued until 1892 when the traffic was prohibited. The importation of live sheep was stopped in 1884, superceded by carcases hung on hooks in insulated holds. The company did not own at this time wharves of its own in the overcrowded area downstream from London Bridge (completed 1831), this came much later, and passengers were embarked at St. Katherine's Wharf completed in 1828. The establishment of a shipbuilding and repair works at Deptford in 1826 meant that the new steamers could be repaired and their sails renewed - a combination of paddle or screw and sails was used well into the 1880s.

By 1828 a service was operating between Portsmouth and Bordeaux, later changed to Southampton - Plymouth - Bordeaux. In much later years when most of the company's routes were cargo only, passenger services remained to Bordeaux, Hamburg and Leith from London. In 1829 the company moved its offices to 71 Lombard Street, a beautiful house which dated from before the Great Fire of London of 1666. By 1830 the company was carrying mails, their packets flying the postal flag, from London to Hamburg, Ostend, Boulogne, Rotterdam, Calais, Antwerp and Havre and from Southampton to Bordeaux. This was helped by the non-existence of any Continental rail services until 1837, with the first British rail link having started

SOHO (foreground) passing the North Foreland on her voyage to Antwerp, ATTWOOD (left) arriving from Newcastle, and WILLIAM JOLLIFFE (right) arriving from Calais. (G.S.N.C. Painting)

between Darlington and Stockton in 1825. The company however frequently transferred ships between routes at this time around 1830 e.g. :-

Attwood (Capt. Stranack) was now operating between London/Rotterdam
Belfast (Capt. Whittingham) was now operating between London/Calais
Brockelbank (Capt. Peart) was now operating between London/Calais
Earl of Liverpool (Capt. Peake) was now operating between London/Ostend
Lord Melville (Capt. Middleton) was now operating between London/Calais
SirEdwardBanks(Capt. Mizon) was now operating between London/Rotterdam
William Jolliffe (Capt. Downie) was now operating between London/Hamburg

There is considerable correspondence in surviving company records of 1831 concerning the paddler *Belfast*, which had been apprehended for smuggling offences both in England and France, resulting in the ultimate dismissal of all of her officers and crew. Much bad publicity had appeared in the newspapers of the time, and the Board in its minutes of December,1831 describes the whole unpleasant affair and their refusal to place any more advertisements in 'The Times'. In addition, delays in the handling of passengers baggage on arrival of *Belfast* at the Custom House Quay led to the recording of 'improper and very colourful Billingsgate remarks' about the company's baggage handler and agent in the minutes. *Talbot* ran aground at Newhaven in 1830 and the minutes record with gratitude the great assistance afforded by Capt. Mingay and the crew of *Hyperion*, and also to the officers and men of the blockade service.

The company entered the London/Granton passenger trade in 1831 with the newly-built *London Merchant*, and acquired their largest yet paddler *Monarch* of length 204 feet in 1833 for this service. She had sleeping accomodation for 140 passengers with 100 of these being able to dine in her saloon at any one time, and *London Merchant* was chartered to the Dundee, Perth & London Shipping Co. Ltd in 1833. The Granton service was expanded by the acquisition of the London & Edinburgh Steam Packet Company in 1836 with six more paddle steamers including *City of Edinburgh, James Watt* and *Tourist* as well as their office in London and a warehouse in Newhaven. The port of Leith was now used by the company for the Edinburgh service, and a new *Leith* was launched on 6th April,1837 from the yard of Menzies & Son at Leith for the service, the event being watched by a large crowd estimated at 40,000 people as she was the largest ever vessel built to date, being 210 feet in length and 907 gross tons and powered by engines of 300 horse power, the previous maximum being 200.

New paddle ships were built for the other services at this time, with *City of Hamburg* (1834) and *John Bull* (1835) for the Hamburg service, and six new paddle steamers in the next year for the Continental routes in *Britannia, Caledonia, Giraffe, Ocean, Clarence* and *Countess of Lonsdale*. *City of Hamburg* sailed on her maiden voyage under the command of Capt. Whittingham, followed by *John Bull* under Capt. Corbin and then in July,1835 by *Britannia* under Capt. Stranack on the Rotterdam service. In 1837 the company owned 40 paddle steamers, a remarkable feat as only one hundred such craft were registered with Lloyd's Register five years earlier, and they also enlarged and improved their shipbuilding and repairing yard at Deptford. The *James Watt* left her Leith route in 1837 to carry the British Legion and its stores from Santander to San Sebastian. The British Legion had been raised in 1836 by Sir de Lacy Evans to help Queen Christina of Spain against the insurrection led by Don Carlos. *Caledonia* was caught smuggling contraband tobacco in 1842, and her greater speed meant she was occasionally used on the Leith service as well as the Hamburg service, and in 1864 she stranded in fog at Flamborough Head and broke up. In 1838 the first iron paddler *Rainbow* joined the fleet, and experiments to solve the deviation of compasses on iron ships were conducted aboard her in the Mersey by Prof. George Biddell Airy, Astronomer Royal, on behalf of the Admiralty. Her passenger accomodation comprised a fore saloon of 43 feet in length, a main saloon of 36 feet in length, a ladies cabin of 18 feet in length and six large deck cabins. She ran first from London to Ramsgate, and then for many years on the Rotterdam and Antwerp services. The second iron steamer in the fleet was *Magician* on the Newhaven/Dieppe run and purchased in 1844.

In 1842 the company gained the royal seal of approval when Queen Victoria travelled aboard *Trident*, built 1841, from Leith to London, having made the London to Leith voyage with Prince Albert on the royal yacht. The historic voyage began after breakfast at 9 a.m. on 15th September,1842 with Lord Liverpool, Lord Hardwicke and the Duchess of Buccleuch in attendance and accompanied by the company's *Monarch*, which had the Queen's horses aboard, as well as other craft. St. Abbs Head was passed at 2 p.m. and Flamborough Head at 5.30 a.m. next day and Yarmouth at 6 p.m. arriving in the Thames at the Nore at 3 a.m. on the 17th. The *Monarch* was the only one of the accompanying ships to keep up with *Trident*, which flew the Royal Standard, one of few times that a ship of the Merchant Navy has done so, Shaw Savill's *Gothic* of 1948 having done this in more recent years for Royal tours of Australasia. Also in 1842 the company's Hull steamer *Vivid*, purchased the year before from the Humber Steamship Company, was in collision with the steamer *Era* in the Thames, the master of the *Vivid* ran her aground on mud but the unfortunate *Era* foundered. *Water Witch* was chartered on 24th June,1843 by the South Eastern Railway Company to mark the latter's railway line reaching Folkestone, and she carried a celebratory party travelling from London to Boulogne and back in one day for the first time. In 1846 *Giraffe* brought over the first live cattle from Rotterdam.

In 1847 the company acquired a lease of part of St. Katherine's Dock just below the Tower of London, and of course some 47 years before the completion of Tower Bridge in 1894 The first company services operated from there to Havre, and soon the dock was to be the major departure point for most of the Continental cargo and passenger services. Excursions down the Thames however still used the upriver Old Swan Pier and London Bridge wharf. In this year of 1847 the company was operating the following main services :-

	Paddle Steamers Employed
Tower of London/Hamburg	Wilberforce,Princess Royal, Countess of Lonsdale, John Bull, Caledonia.
Brown's Wharf(Poplar)/Leith	Trident, Clarence, Leith
Blackwall/Rotterdam & Antwerp	Rainbow, Giraffe, Ocean
Blackwall/Ostend	Triton, Sir Edward Banks, Venezuela
London Bridge Wharf/Hull	Vivid, Water Witch
London Bridge Wharf/Calais	Belfast, Tourist, Earl of Liverpool
St. Katherine's Wharf/Havre	James Watt, Columbine
London Bridge Wharf/Boulogne	Star, Harlequin, William Jolliffe
Wapping/Newcastle	London Merchant, City of Hamburg
Brighton/Dieppe	Menai, Fame
Dover/Boulogne	Magician, City of London
Margate/Ramsgate excursions	Eagle, Attwood, Magnet, Ramona, Mercury, Little Western.
Southampton/Bordeaux	Lion

Magician was purchased in May,1844 for the Dover to Calais and Boulogne service and soon after the *City of London* joined her on this service, which ran until 1850. The 1851 opening of the Great Exhibition in Hyde Park brought a great increase in passengers visiting London aboard the company's ships. The exhibition's magnificent Crystal Palace of ornate iron and glass was designed by Joseph Paxton and featured 13,800 exhibits proudly showing off the best that Britain could offer from the Industrial Revolution. The Palace was removed to Sydenham at the exhibition's conclusion and later in 1936 was destroyed by fire. A Government survey in 1853 of leading steam packet companies operating from the Thames showed 134 steamers in operation, with 59 wooden paddlers, 52 iron paddlers and 23 iron screw steamers. Fifty of these were owned by the company, including six paddle corvettes purchased that year from the Germanic Confederation complete with stores and guns, being part of the German Navy of the day, the remainder being three paddle frigates including the famous former Cunarders *Britannia* and *Acadia* of 1839 and 1840, and two sail frigates.

At this time, the British deep-sea steam-driven fleet was of around the same size, consisting of both paddlers and screw-driven ships, and principally in the fleets of the Peninsular & Oriental Steam Navigation (P. & O.), Cunard, Royal Mail and Pacific Steam Navigation Companies. The first iron hulled and the first screw-propelled ship to cross the Atlantic had been Brunel's *Great Britain* of 3270 grt, launched on 19th July,1843 from the Patterson yard at Bristol and which made her historic voyage on 26th July,1845 for New York. Shorter experimental voyages with a variety of screws had been made earlier by smaller ships such as *Archimedes* of 240 tons built in 1838 and which circumnavigated the British Isles in 1840. The great P. & O. company had been founded on 22nd August,1837 as the Peninsular Steam Navigation Company for the route to Spain and Portugal by Brodie Willcox and Arthur Anderson. Their first ship *Don Juan* sailed on 1st September,1837 but she was wrecked on the 15th of that month at Tarifa on the first homeward voyage from Gibraltar, she was carrying mails and a large amount of cash. 1839 saw the award of the Egypt mail contract and the setting up of the Peninsular & Oriental Steam Navigation Company, which received its Royal Charter in 1840. 1842 saw the award of the India mail contract, and services were extended to Singapore and Hong Kong in 1845 and to Australia in 1852. The importance of the company in this book is that the great coastal empire of General Steam was taken over by P. & O. in 1920. Their finest and newest ship in 1853 was the *Himalaya* of 3438 grt completed at Blackwall that year by C. J. Mare for the London to Alexandria service. She steamed at 13.5 knots with the mails, which were carried overland in Egypt to Suez for the connecting India steamers until the Suez Canal was opened in 1869.

General Steam was justifiably proud of its service between London and Hamburg, with *Tourist* taking only 59 hours in the 1830s 'including all stoppages and against a head wind'. On the strength of this, an offer was made to carry the mails to Hamburg to the Postmaster-General, who was in communication at the highest level with the Chancellor of the Exchequer before the offer was accepted. Thus the early company paddle steamers carried the mails on a fairly regular basis, and the efficiency of their private operation persuaded the Admiralty to hand over the carriage of mails to private shipping companies from the mid-1840s (and to the railway companies from 1863). The busy Weymouth/Channel Islands, Irish Sea routes and Dover/Calais mail services were all privatised by 1854. The Admiralty had taken over from the Post Office steam packets in 1837 after large financial losses had been suffered by the latter, whose steam packet operation dated back to 1821 and whose sailing cutters had carried the mails to the Continent and Ireland since the middle of the previous century.

The company was very much a family-oriented company at this time, with the surnames of its long-serving Masters being repeatedly mentioned as they transferred from one route to another at regular intervals. The directors also held long-time appointments and descendants of Thomas Brockelbank including Kathleen G. Brockelbank were still living in the family Greenwich home after the turn of the 20th century. Names of other employees are frequently repeated in company rolls particularly at the Deptford shipyard including Westwood, Littlewood, Black, Guy, Carter, Hayward, Hall, Howgego, Kimber, Robinson and many others.

One interesting and true story of this period relates to the charter during 1833 of two of the company's ships by the Queen Regnant of Portugal in her bid to regain the throne during a civil war. They were part of a squadron of supply ships supporting the warships commanded by one of Admiral Nelson's former Captains at the Battle of Trafalgar, Capt. Napier. His plan was to embark troops at Oporto and take them south to invade southern Portugal, and he was completely successful in restoring the Queen to her throne. On his returning the ships in very good condition to the company, a letter was sent to the Captain from the company complimenting him on that fact, and this letter is still in existence today, having been kept by the company's agent in Oporto all through the years, including its removal to London for safekeeping during World War II.

IRON-HULLED SCREW STEAMERS

General Steam's first screw-propelled ship was the *Dragon* of 535 grt completed on the Tyne in 1853 at the Palmer yard in Jarrow for the London to Newcastle service, and was followed later the same year by the similar *Pilot* and *Pioneer*, the latter to run with *Dragon* under Capt. Wade and *Wansbeck* of 1857 on the Newcastle service. *Pilot* under the command of Capt. Vaughan was used on the London to Boulogne service. In 1854 England and France declared war on Russia and the Crimean campaign in the Black Sea began. In the following year the company's wooden steam paddler *Edinburgh* of 741 grt was chartered by the French Government for transport service. Many ships were sent out to the Crimeam War as transports, one such was *Arno* which was also used as a military store ship at Eupatoria, and later purchased by the company in 1861. In 1856 screw-propelled ships were introduced to the Leith service for the first time, and the paddle excursion ship *Eagle* completed at Northfleet in 1853 was purchased for the Ramsgate and Margate service. She could carry 466 passengers at nearly 15 knots and was a great favourite until sold thirty years later. Recollections of the company's paddle steamers around 1860 were made by W. L. Wyllie in the company's centenary book published in 1924, and offer a valuable insight into London river of the time :-

'The oldest paddle steamer was the *Rainbow* of 1838, which had been the company's first iron steamer. She had long arms working up from below through the bridge into the open air, and the engines sang quite a pleasant song as they worked up and down. The ship had a low freeboard and was more yacht-like than her younger consorts *Cologne*, *Concordia*, *Panther*, *Rhine*, *Seine* and *Moselle* of 1852, and which operated services to Hamburg, Rotterdam, Boulogne, Ostend, Calais and Havre. We children got to know the London river almost by heart as we travelled up and down year after year - what a change to the present day! In 1860 the North East collier brigs lay four and six deep in tiers on both sides of the waterway. The drifting barges drove upstream as thick as bees. When our warps were slipped at London Bridge, our stout old paddle steamer would force her way through the throng, giving a push here, and a nudge there, now and then turning astern and sending the

FALCON of 1876 (above) was built by Charles Mitchell on the Tyne at Low Walker and had a career with the company that spanned fifty years. She was their first ship to enter Hamburg in 1919 after the end of the Great War. LAPWING of 1879 (below) sails down the Thames after passing through Tower Bridge. She was built by Gourlay of Dundee and after her sale in 1911 she had a long second career under the Turkish flag.

drifting barges broadside on into the press with the wash of her paddles, or making a cannon off a tier of craft'.

'The bluff-bowed old colliers were backing and filling their sails in the fairway, and the jumping coal whippers were whisking baskets of black diamonds from many a dusty hold. Soon the jostling pool is left behind, and in the wider reaches we meet the tea clippers and Cape Horners hurrying on the flood, escorted by fussy tugs. Fish carriers from the North Sea work their way towards Billingsgate. Topsail barges are everywhere, some almost awash and others flying light or piled halfmast high with straw and hay. Our ship *Panther* under Capt. Balleston keeps up a steady 12 knots and soon the old *Dreadnought*, one of Nelson's ships at Trafalgar, and now a hospital for seamen comes into sight; just beyond are the two towers of Greenwich and the Observatory on the hill above. Here in the stream is a boy's training ship. *Eagle*, carrying crowds of holiday makers, overtakes us, giving a whiff of cigars and cheap scent as she passes to windward, with sounds of a merry polka and the stamp of feet, and she rounds Blackwall Point leaving a track of glistening foam. The big liners, which all carried sail at this time, would be met and towed out of the dock entrances, and worked their way down against the last of the flood. Here are sailing ships crowded with emigrants - shepherds with their dogs, farm-hands, gold diggers off to Australia, and children, wives and sweethearts'.

The graphic descriptions of W. L. Wyllie go on to depict a voyage home from Boulogne on a company ship with an unpleasant cargo of pigs. He remembered one company paddle steamer in a gale trying to make harbour at Boulogne - 'A strong flood tide was running across the entrance, and big breakers broke upon the bar continually. Just as the stout old paddle boat was running for the calm water between the pier heads, a huge wave rose astern of her, broaching her to. In a moment she was broadside on right in the middle of the furious breakers. Things looked very bad, but the stout old skipper kept his head, brought his ship head to sea, and took her out into the deep water, where he turned once more and ran safely into shelter'.

Another colourful character born into the busy Thames scenes of 1863 was the author's great grandfather Capt. Henry Norman, whose first ship was the company's *Libra* of 1869 on the Hamburg run. He was born the son of an Army farrier within the sound of Bow Bells, but in his early 'teens with both parents dead he had to look after himself. He worked for a few months as a draper's assistant, sleeping under the shop bench at night, before beginning his apprenticeship with the company. The sights of London river, such as the twin domes of Greenwich with the Observatory on the hill above, and the busy traffic with queues of ships waiting to enter the locks leading to the enclosed docks, became second nature to him. He switched to Cory's colliers in 1886, joining the *Stelling* and a long succession of colliers and in command of *Northumbria, Devereux* and *Ocean*. He was Cory Commodore of the latter ship when she was torpedoed off Hartlepool in 1917. Capt. Norman, who was asleep in his cabin when the torpedo struck, had a narrow escape from being trapped, and suffered shoulder injuries in trying to force a way out. He resumed as Cory Commodore at the end of the war, retiring in 1927 when his last command *Corbrook* was sold. He had fond memories of the Cory steam tugs on the Thames, the first of which was operational in 1859, and particularly the 'toshers', one-man operated tugs used to move barges of which an example, *Varlet*, is preserved today at Gravesend. The same word was used in the 'Navvies' context by their Mediterranean seafarers when describing home trade vessels.

The company from 1864 began to mostly use a nomenclature of bird names for their ships, the first being *Stork* of 843 grt built that year by Gourlay at Dundee, and the purchased *Heron* of 624 grt built in 1860 at Dumbarton. In 1865 with the cattle trade from the Continent flourishing, the company built the iron paddler *Taurus* of 838 grt at Preston Iron Works, equipping her with wooden pens. She carried 650 head of cattle and about 500 sheep, and voyaged weekly between Hamburg and Tonning in Schleswig-Holstein and London for many years at 14 knots without the loss of a single animal. A model of her was kept in the South Kensington Museum for thirty years. An outbreak of cattle plague on the Continent in 1866 seriously affected the company's trade. In 1870 northern Continental ports were blocked by ice, and the Franco - German war began. In 1872 the company's profits fell as the price of coal and stores and wages rose. The capital of the company was increased in 1873, and in 1874 it obtained a further Act of Parliament extending its powers and consolidating previous Acts. In 1876 two new services to Amsterdam and Harlingen began, and the Bordeaux service was restarted.

The *Penguin* of 1876 carried a notable cargo in 1878 after the Franco - German War. Under Capt. J. S. Marshall she was laden with a quarter of a million of the famous Spandau sovereigns, which she carried to Hamburg as payment from the French. At the mouth of the Elbe, a fog descended and *Penguin* dropped anchor. As she was getting under way a German steamer ran into her, cutting into her aft-hold some three inches above the waterline, and penetrating to within three inches of the bullion. *Penguin* was listed to make her seaworthy and she proceeded to Hamburg to unload her valuable cargo, which was taken intact to Spandau castle. Homeward cargo from Germany included sugar packed in bags and cases, toys from Bavaria, glassware, surgical appliances, sugar beet and fruit. The company occasionally carried wild animals to and from Hagenbeck's circus at Hamburg. Dutch cargoes included edam and gouda cheese, sugar, liquers, butter and margarine, Spring bulbs of every shade of colour from the fields of Haarlem. Tea and tobacco from the Dutch colonies was also transshipped at Rotterdam for London. Live eels were another strange cargo, which on arrival in the Thames were discharged into lighters and carried to the Dutch eel boats or scuyts anchored off Billingsgate fish market.

RATIONALISATION OF PASSENGER SERVICES

By 1880, the growth of the railway companies fleets had reached such a point that the cross-Channel passengers carried by the company on its important French/Belgian services had seriously diminished, and the company's main passenger routes had become those to Leith, Hamburg and Bordeaux. This was as a result of the 1863 Government decree that empowered all railway companies to own and operate their own vessels, although each route had still to be applied for and be operated. Shortly afterwards, three competing railway companies were operating out of Dover, Folkestone and Newhaven, with the Great Eastern Railway operating out of Harwich although Parkeston Quay did not open until 1883, and the Great Western Railway was operating out of Weymouth by 1878. In 1880 the company fleet stood at its greatest ever strength of 60 steamers of 41,102 grt, and the smaller number of passengers travelling on routes such as those to Rotterdam and Antwerp were then accomodated on the cargo ships. The main passenger services were now to :-

1. **LEITH**
2. **BORDEAUX**
3. **HAMBURG**
4. **OSTEND**
5. **SUMMER EXCURSIONS**

LEITH In 1888 the Leith passenger service received the fast new steamer *Seamew* of 1543 grt from the Palmer yard on the Tyne with accomodation for over 100 passengers in three classes. She was a development of *Albatross* of 1884 which had a considerable passenger capacity. The builders model in the National Maritime Museum shows a well-decked vessel with hinged bulwarks for easy cargo loading i.e. a flush-decked vessel when seen out at sea from abeam. She had central passenger and bridge accomodation, and houses on the poop for the crew. The company ran three weekly passenger sailings but faced stiff competition from four other companies on the Leith passenger route, and did not resume passenger sailings after the Great War. In an interesting footnote to these East Coast services, during the 19th century Customs

COMPETITORS ON LEITH SERVICE

London & Edinburgh Shipping Co. Ltd founded in Leith in 1809 when it acquired the Leith smacks of the Union Company, being superseded by schooners and clippers and finally to steam in 1852. It provided the greatest competition to General Steam with three weekly passenger sailings from its ten-strong fleet including four passenger ships of 1200 grt. Passenger sailings continued after the Great War and two fine passenger ships of 2200 grt were built as *Royal Fusilier* in 1924 and *Royal Archer* in 1928 with accomodation for passengers. The three-ship fleet in 1939 were all sunk during the war. In 1945 General Steam together with the London & Edinburgh Shipping Co. Ltd, the Carron Company and the Clyde Shipping Co. Ltd, formed London Scottish Lines Ltd to carry on cargo trade between the Firth of Forth and London and between the Clyde and London. A cargo-only service was run to London until 1958.

Carron Company of Falkirk founded in the 18th century. Their black funnelled ships ran passenger services from Grangemouth to London, where they berthed on the Carron wharf at St. Katharine's Dock just below Tower Bridge, the latter completed in 1894. They ran three weekly sailings from Grangemouth with an additional weekly one from Granton. Their steamers were named after rivers such as *Forth* of 1886, *Thames* of 1887 and *Avon* of 1897. Their regular passenger services to London were discontinued in the inter-war years.

Dundee, Perth & London Shipping Co. Ltd founded in 1826 and provided passenger sailings to London from Dundee continuously from 1834 to 1939 with only a brief resumption during 1946. Three weekly passenger services were operated, and the last new passenger-carrying ship built for the company was *Dundee* of 1541 grt from the Caledon yard in 1934 with accomodation for 12 passengers, which ran with *London* of 1921 with accomodation for 30 passengers and *Perth* of 1915 with accomodation for 208 passengers. The last coastal passengers on the East Coast were carried for a brief few months in 1946 by *Aboyne* of 1937 which was then sold to the Clyde Shipping Co. Ltd. A cargo-only service ran until discontinued in November,1961 by this well-remembered company, whose steamers had red funnels with black tops.

Aberdeen Steam Navigation Co. Ltd founded in 1821 with sailing smacks. The first paddle steamer was *Queen of Scotland* built at Aberdeen in 1828 for the company. The company was incorporated in 1918 and their buff-funnelled steamers sailed twice-weekly to London. Swift was sold by GSNC to the company in 1927 to become *Harlaw*. The shares were purchased by the Tyne-Tees Shipping Co. Ltd in 1945 and thus passed under the control of Coast Lines, and the London passenger service ceased in 1947/48.

WOODCOCK of 1906 (above) was used on the London to Leith route of the company. She was built at Dundee by Gourlay and sold in 1926 to Italian owners and renamed OTRANTO. She foundered off Northern Luzon, Philippines on 20th March,1934 while on a voyage from Venice to Shanghai. FAUVETTE of 1912 (below) was built by Sir Raylton Dixon & Co. Ltd on Teesside and was a 'well-decker' with hinged bulwarks for quick unloading of horses and cattle. She became a war loss on 9th March,1916.

baggage checks were made when the vessels docked at Tilbury from Leith, so most passengers stayed on board and disembarked at St. Katharine's Wharf where no checks were made ! Scotland has only just received a separate parliament again in 1997, the last being in 1707, and why customs checks were necessary remains a mystery.

BORDEAUX In 1890 the General Steam passenger service to Bordeaux received the fast new steamer *Hirondelle* of 1607 grt from the Gourlay yard at Dundee with accomodation for 145 passengers in three classes. She appeared to be a flush-decker but on closer examination there was a 30 feet long well-deck in front of the bridge formed by outward swinging hinged doors flush with the bulwarks. She had a patented system for controlling her watertight doors on her bulkheads. A model of this system was exhibited at the Paris Exhibition of 1900, where it was awarded a Gold Medal for life-saving at sea. She was a development of *Seamew* of 1888, and her first class cabins and public rooms were situated at the aft of the long main deck, second-class were at the forward end and third class under the fo'c'stle. She was transferred to Harwich/Hamburg route in 1905 and in 1914 to the London/Leith route. The company passenger service to Bordeaux was not resumed after the Great War. The little ancient port of Tonnay - Charente on the Cognac river to the north of the Gironde exported brandy and cognac to London, and three-quarters of this trade was carried in company vessels. Other Bordeaux cargo included fresh plums in summer (prunes in winter) as well as wine, brandy, pears, rosin, turpentine, talc, tartars, walnuts, tanning extract and wool from Mazamet. British wool was carried to Bordeaux on the company's ships and then sent by rail to Mazamet, where they were washed in the local waters to make them soft and returned to Bordeaux for import to Hull on the company's ships for the Yorkshire mills.

HAMBURG In 1888 the company passenger service to Hamburg was transferred from London to Parkeston Quay at Harwich, the first sailing being taken by *Hawk* of 1876 on 29th March. In 1891 this passenger service to Hamburg received the fast new steamer *Peregrine* of 1664 grt from the W. B Thompson yard at Dundee with accomodation for around 200 passengers, an improvement on the elderly company steamers built around 1870 which carried only 150 passengers on the twice-weekly service. However she completed only one round voyage to Hamburg before she was sold to Howard Smith Ltd of Melbourne for Australian coastal passenger services. She was replaced by an iron-hulled ship of the same name from the same yard a year later, which ran from Harwich to Hamburg until the outbreak of war when she became a flotilla supply ship. She was not a well-decker and was returned to the company in

MAVIS of 1888 (above) was one of five excursion paddle steamers built by J. Scott & Co. of Kinghorn for the company. She was sold in 1910 to Pockett's Bristol Channel Steam Packet Co. Ltd and broken up at Briton Ferry in 1915. (A. Duncan)

GOLDEN EAGLE of 1909 was probably the most famous of the company's excursion steamers. After long excursion service and arduous war service in two World Wars, her last summer season was in 1949, and in 1951 she was taken to Grays in Essex for breaking up. (Real Photos)

ALOUETTE (above) was built by Denny in 1894 as CALVADOS for the London, Brighton & South Coast Railway Company. She was purchased in 1901 for London to Ostend passenger and cargo service and was broken up at Rainham in 1924. (A. Duncan)

KELVINSIDE of 1893 (below) was built as HARE. She entered the fleet in 1906 from J. Crisp & Son of Great Yarmouth when that company was taken over, and was sold for further service in 1922 and broken up in 1933.

1915 but was unfortunately wrecked near the Sunk Light Vessel on 29th December,1917. Her running partners on the route included *Gannet* of 1878, *Lapwing* of 1879 with *Seamew* of 1888 transferred from the Leith route at the turn of the century. The company passenger service to Hamburg was not resumed after the Great War.

OSTEND. The last passenger and cargo-carrying paddle steamers built for the company were the iron-hulled sisters *Swallow* and *Swift* of 1875 for the Ostend run. They were of 625 grt and built by Pearce of Stockton, and were the last pair of a formidable total of 38 new paddle steamers built for or purchased by the company since 1850. An amusing story is told of the Master of one of this last pair of company paddlers, who took a great interest in astronomy, his passengers having to suffer long colloquys on the subject at his dinner table. Passports were not necessary at this time to establish identity, and a 'Mr. Smith' was invited to the Captain's table, and proved to be a most attentive listener throughout the conversation. Only after 'Mr. Smith' had left the ship did the Master find out that his guest was none other than the Astronomer Royal. In 1901 the London/Ostend service was updated with the arrival of the *Alouette* (French for *'Swallow'*) built in 1894 and recently purchased, replacing the two paddle steamers *Swallow* and *Swift* after 26 years on the route. *Alouette* was requisitioned at the start of the Great War and served around Scapa Flow. She was returned to the company on 21st November,1919 and served for a further four years before being sold for breaking up at Rainham in 1924.

SUMMER EXCURSIONS TO MARGATE, RAMSGATE, CLACTON & YARMOUTH The Margate and Ramsgate excursions were run by *Eagle* of 1853, *Hoboken* of 1873 built as an Elbe tender for the Adler Line and purchased in 1877, and by the iron paddler *Hilda* under Capt. Fishenden. The latter had been built in 1862 as *Eugenie* by Samuelson of Hull for the South Eastern Railway Company and was renamed *Cornubia* in 1863 and purchased in 1868 and renamed *Hilda*. She was the first twin-funneller in the fleet, the next was in 1929, and she was broken up in 1889. This excursion trio were replaced by five new paddle steamers of 550 grt constructed by J. Scott at Kinghorn between 1887 and 1889 and named *Halcyon, Mavis, Oriole, Laverock* and *Philomel*, which ran day excursions to the Kent coast and to France at 18.5 knots particularly in 1889 for the Paris Exhibition of that year. They were also built to operate during the summer months from June on the excursions from London Bridge and the other landings down to Tilbury to Clacton and Great Yarmouth, which was just beginning to expand as a resort. Passengers stayed overnight at hotels in Yarmouth and returned the next day, leaving at 8 a.m. After the rival 'Belle' steamers came into operation around 1890, the hulls and funnels of the new excursion quintet were changed from black to buff with a black band being added to the funnel at a later date. The Yarmouth service continued until 1905, with the last of the quintet *Oriole* being sold to Dutch owners in 1912.

The competition to the company in the Thames excursion trades was considerable at the turn of the century, with seven paddle steamers completed by the famous Denny yard at Dumbarton for Belle Steamers between 1890 and 1898, and three large and famous paddlers built for Palace Steamers during that decade. The first of the latter trio was *Koh-i-Noor* of 884 grt built in 1892 by the Fairfield yard on the Clyde, *Royal Sovereign* of 891 grt completed by the same yard in 1893, and the larger and more luxurious *La Marguerite* of 1554 grt again from the Fairfield yard. All of the trio were 20-knot steamers carrying up to two thousand passengers, and provided formidable opposition to the company. However this was eventually overcome, with *La Marguerite*, the largest paddler ever to operate on the Thames, sold in 1904 for North Wales service, *Koh-i-Noor* broken up in 1919 and *Royal Sovereign* purchased by the company in 1929. Belle Steamers had disposed of the majority of their fleet by 1922 with three, *Walton Belle, Yarmouth Belle* and *Woolwich Belle*, being purchased by the New Medway Steam Packet Co. Ltd, which was itself taken over by the company in 1936. In addition, *Southend Belle* was purchased as *Laguna Belle* by the company in 1935.

MEDITERRANEAN AND FURTHER AFIELD

In 1882 the company established a service to the west coast of Italy and Sicily, which was to be the basis of their Mediterranean service for the next eighty years. Ports served included Catania, Civitavecchia, Genoa, Livorno, Messina, Naples, Palermo, Pozzuoli, Savona, Spezia and Syracuse. In the same year the Government chartered several company ships for the Egyptian Transport Service. *Osprey* under Capt. Taylor made a quick passage from London to Alexandria as a troopship, and *Libra* and *Nautilus* were also to be found in the Mediterranean that year. The larger company ships were reserved for the Mediterranean trade which was extended to Patras in Greece and Izmir and Istanbul in Turkey. *Albatross* built by Palmer in 1884 of 1450 grt was typical of the larger type of ship used on the Mediterranean services. She was a well-decker and traded from London to Hamburg or Bordeaux but was also employed on the Mediterranean service mainly to West Italian ports and Sicily. She made a passage on charter to the British Government from London to Suakin (Sudan) via Malta in 1885, the year of General Gordon's death during the Sudan troubles. She and four other company ships *Cygnet, Raven, Guilemot* and *Linnet* made a total of eighteen voyages to West Africa during 1894/95 when the company tried unsuccessfully to gain a foothold in the Manchester and Liverpool trade to West Africa. She sailed on her first voyage to West African ports from Liverpool on 7th March,1894 arriving back in Liverpool on 23rd May. Her fifth and last voyage to Freetown and Lagos and the many ports in between was from Liverpool on 13th April,1895 arriving back there on 11th July,1895. She then resumed her normal Mediterranean service from Newcastle and London to Genoa. She may have carried a few passengers to West Africa as she certainly carried some when on Mediterranean or the Bordeaux services. She was given new boilers in 1907 and sold off in 1923.

The Mediterranean cargo ships usually carried no more than a dozen passengers, and loaded at Newcastle and Middlesbrough as well as London, and called at Newlyn and Penzance from time to time when outward bound to

RAVEN of 1883 (above) was built at Stockton, and is seen arriving at Bristol from the Mediterranean. She was also used on the West African service in 1894/95 and was broken up in 1914. HIRONDELLE of 1890 (below) was used on the Bordeaux service. She was built by Gourlay of Dundee and became a war loss on 25th April,1917.

load salted fish in barrels for the Italian market. The impressive volcanic rock of Gibraltar, named after the Arab conqueror Gibel Tarik, and its opposite Pillar of Hercules - Abyla on the North African coast - meant warmer weather and calmer seas for the 'Navvies' However, this was not without its dangers, as in 1883 the Mediterranean trades were seriously affected by the outbreak of cholera in Southern France, Spain and Italy. Trade was so bad by 1886 that reductions in office staff salaries and directors fees were made. The iron-hulled *Raven* of 1883 by Pearce of Stockton and the similar sized steel-hulled *Cygnet* of 1883 by Gourlay of Dundee were two of the first ships used by the company to the Mediterranean. Both were lengthened by 36 feet in 1892 to 286 feet length overall and increased their grt to around 2,000. *Raven* made a total of four voyages to West Africa in 1894/95, her first was from Liverpool on 30th March,1894 arriving back in Manchester on 10th July. Her last voyage to West Africa commenced on 4th March,1895 from Liverpool, arriving back there on 14th June, resuming her normal trade from London to the Mediterranean later that month, and she was broken up in 1914. *Cygnet* mainly traded to Patras (Greece) and Smyrna (Turkey) as well as the usual range of Italian ports and was also employed for five voyages on the West African service in 1894/95, her first voyage was from Liverpool on 15th February,1894 to Sierra Leone and Lagos and Accra arriving back at Liverpool on 7th May. Her last West African voyage was from Liverpool on 4th May,1895 arriving back there on 5th August and left for London via Penarth to restart her Mediterranean service to Messina and other Italian ports. She was lost in December,1903 as a result of an explosion and fire in her cargo en route to the Mediterranean.

Linnet of 1890 was built as *Dieppois* for French owners by the Campbeltown Shipbuilding Company and was purchased in 1892. As well as trading to the the Mediterranean, she made three voyages to West Africa in 1894/95, the first leaving from Liverpool on 30th October,1894 and the last on 27th March,1895 arriving back on 1st July. Her next voyage was from Liverpool to the Black Sea, sailing on 10th July and also loading at Maryport before arriving at Bourgas in Bulgaria some 17 days later. She was damaged by fire in August,1901 and sold to Uruguayan owners. *Guillemot* of 1894 was an exact sister of *Linnet* and from the same yard, obviously ordered by the company when pleased with their purchase of her sister from French owners. After running her trials, she sailed for Liverpool where she loaded for West Africa, sailing from Liverpool on 1st May on her maiden voyage arriving back at Dunkirk on 26th August. Her next voyage was from Liverpool to Bilbao on 22nd September, and on her return in the ensuing years she traded to the Mediterranean and Black Sea from the Tyne, Tees and London. She made a

SHELDRAKE of 1894 was built as KELVINGROVE by Osborne, Graham & Co. of Sunderland for J. Black of Glasgow. She was purchased in 1898 and had an interesting career with the company on voyages to Galveston and to South America on charter, and on her regular Mediterranean route. She was sunk near Marittimo Island, Italy by U34 on 8th November,1916 while on a voyage from Naples to London. PEREGRINE of 1892 (below) was built by W. B. Thompson & Co. at Dundee, her namesake of the previous year from the same builder having been sold to Australian owners. She ran to Hamburg from Harwich for the company and was wrecked near the Sunk Light Ship on 29th December,1917 while on a voyage from Rotterdam to Harwich.

good passage fully loaded in 1895 from Taganrog on the Azov Sea to Plymouth, and was an occasional vistor to Adriatic ports including Venice and Fiume (Rijeka). She foundered and was lost in December,1911.

Adjutant of 2394 grt completed by the William Gray yard at West Hartlepool in 1893 was a new ship for the Medierranean trade, with homeward cargoes offering ore, fruits and vegetables of all kinds, cheese and olive oil, while outward cargoes included fish, machinery and spare parts, and general cargo of all kinds. She traded to Italy and was a frequent visitor to the Black Sea especially Taganrog e.g. Taganrog to Bergen in 1901, Theodosia to Copenhagen in 1897, Smyrna to Bristol in 1895. On 10th January,1894 she left Barry for Buenos Aires with coal on charter, arriving at Montevideo on 10th February and Rosario on 5th March, and she subsequently left with grain for Rotterdam calling at St. Vincent (Cape Verde) on 14th April and arrived at Maasluis on 28th April. Her next deepwater voyage was with coal from the Tyne on 3rd December,1895 for Buenos Aires passing Dover on 6th December and arrived at San Lorenzo near Rosario on on 5th February,1896. She left Rosario with grain on 15th February arriving in the Bristol Channel on 8th April and docking at Sharpness (Gloucester) on 11th April. She made a Transatlantic voyage from Sunderland on 1st June,1898 arriving at Philadelphia later that month and sailing on 24th June for Dublin where she arrived on 12th July. She then moved across the Irish Sea to Whitehaven and round to the Tyne, Tees and London to resume her Mediterranean trading. She was lost by collision off Deal en route to Naples on 22nd October,1914 with Prince Line's *Ocean Prince* of 1907, which suffered little damage and was able to continue her voyage.

The failure of the company's attempt to enter the established Manchester and Liverpool trade to West Africa against the established Sir Alfred Jones and Elder,Dempster & Company in 1894 compounded a serious financial situation. The dock labourers' strike of 1889 had increased costs, and with the cessation of the Continental cattle trade in 1892, which had provided £74,930 of net receipts only ten years earlier, the worst trading years of the company were from 1892 until 1895, with the fleet falling in strength from the fifty owned steamers in 1890. The company accounts for 1893/94 show a gross profit of £23,000 for the half year, but no less than £20,000 of this had to be transferred to the insurance account to pay for shipping casualties. The *Kestrel* was run down in the Elbe, and the amount recovered was less than one-third of the company's loss, while two other serious collisions occurred, one between two of the company's steamers, and the other between the *Rainbow* and the German steamer *Falke*, for which both ships were held to blame. The result was that only £1,618 of the gross profit was able to be carried forward to the next year. The directors at this point saw the future direction of the company to be in the chartering out of the larger ships, as shown by the voyages with coal from the Tyne to Buenos Aires in 1898. No new cargo ships were built for the company from 1895 until 1902 as a consequence of the financial situation, however eight much cheaper second-hand ships were purchased including two of over 2,000 grt for the Mediterranean trade, *Sheldrake* built in 1894 and purchased early in 1898 as *Kelvingrove*, and *Preston* built in 1885 for Sir Robert Ropner of West Hartlepool and purchased in 1899.

Kelvingrove was purchased from John Black & Company of Glasgow, sailing ship owners, for whom she was their first steamer and had been less than successful. She had been built by Osborne, Graham & Company of Sunderland and most of her voyages for her original owner were to Galveston (Texas) and Argentina, mainly from London but also from Hull, Tyne, Newport and other ports. After she was acquired she made further voyages to Galveston calling at Wilmington in North Carolina and Brunswick in Georgia and at New York, other voyages being made on charter to South America in 1898. Some of her return voyages from Galveston included calling at Halifax(NS) for London, a call at Pensacola in the Gulf of Mexico returning to Antwerp via Norfolk (Va) and suffering 'sundry heavy weather damage in the North Atlantic', and a call at New York returning to Bordeaux during the same year. Her last Galveston voyage was from Barry on 23rd November,1898 returning to Antwerp on 8th February,1899. She then loaded at London and called at Cardiff on 3rd March,1899 for Venice and on her return to the U.K. was renamed *Sheldrake*. She later left the Tyne with coal on 17th June,1900 for Halifax(NS) arriving on 2nd July, sailing four days later and arriving back at Preston on 1st August. She made a Mediterranean voyage and then left the Tyne again with coal for Galveston on 8th November,1900 arriving on 4th December. She left there a week later for Hamburg, calling at Norfolk (Va) but unfortunately ran aground in the Elbe and had to be lightened by removal of some of her cargo and finally docked at Hamburg on 18th January,1901. She sailed down the Elbe on 5th February,1901 for Halifax(NS) via the Tees, and left the Nova Scotian port on 28th February,1901 to arrive back in the Thames on 29th March,1901, having been anchored in the The Downs for a week. She then traded regularly to Italy, Sicily, North Africa (Tunis/Oran) and to Kertch in the Sea of Azov. She later became a war loss in November,1916 when she was captured and sunk by U34 near Marittimo Island, Italy while on a voyage from Naples to London.

The company's involvement in the deep water trades to West Africa, South America and to Galveston had thus occupied a seven year period from 1894 to 1901. *Preston* of 2099 grt was purchased in 1899 from Sir Robert Ropner and had been named after his Stockton mansion, which today is the major tourist attraction of Preston Park. She had been completed by Matthew Pearce of Stockton in November, 1885 for worldwide tramping, and after seven years of Mediterranean trading for the company was wrecked on 2nd May, 1906 at Point Bay near Camarinas while on a voyage from London to Genoa with general cargo. Other vessels purchased from British tramp owners included *Tintern Abbey* from Pyman, Watson & Co. Ltd of Newport in 1899 and renamed *Auk*, *Merannio* from Glasgow tramp owners Maclay & McIntyre in 1901, and *Vesuvio* from the Mossgiel Steamship Co. Ltd of Glasgow in 1900, having been built for liner owners Ben Line of Leith as *Czar* in 1879, and *Balgownie* in 1901 having been built for the Grampian Steamship Co. Ltd in 1880.

A NEW CENTURY

The company entered the new century snugly settled into new premises at Great Tower Street, well-placed with a large fleet of 48 steamers for their many short-sea and Mediterranean trades. The company's summer Thames excursion trade still had huge numbers of customers, and had been boosted in 1898 by the delivery from Gourlay Brothers of Dundee of the third *Eagle*, of length 265 feet and of 647 grt and a speed of 18 knots. This was in part to fight off heavy competition from Belle Steamers and New Palace Steamers, and in particular from the Victoria Steamboat Association, formed specifically to break the monopoly of the company. *Eagle* served the three resorts of Southend, Margate and Ramsgate, sailing from London Bridge wharf around 0900 and reaching Southend around 1130 after calling to pick up more passengers at Greenwich, Woolwich and Tilbury. Margate was reached at 1330 and Ramsgate at 1420 with 45 minutes ashore at the latter resort before reboarding her passengers, and calling at Margate at 1600 and Southend at 1730 on the return trip before arriving back at London Bridge around 2000 hours. There was also an express steamer which left London Bridge wharf at 0845 hours for Margate and Ramsgate. *Eagle* also inaugurated a new route which sailed on from Ramsgate to Deal and Dover, and she was joined in 1906 by the turbine-powered triple-screw *Kingfisher* of 982 grt from Denny on the Clyde. *Halcyon* and *Kingfisher* ran from Tilbury on cross-Channel excursions to Boulogne at over 20 knots, but the latter's speed on the Thames brought a host of insurance claims from small craft swamped by her wash, and her lack of manoeuvrablity at piers forced a return to paddles with another new paddle steamer in 1909, *Golden Eagle* of 793 grt from John Brown at Clydebank, powered by triple-expansion steam engines, the first Thames pleasure steamer to be powered in that way. She was equipped with a wheel on the fo'c'stle to steer a bow rudder, essential for excursion ships which proceeded to upriver berths stern first to avoid difficulties of turning in the river. *Kingfisher* was

STORK of 1904 was built by Ropner at Stockton and was a mainstay of the company's Mediterranean services for over thirty years until she arrived at Blyth for breaking up at the end of March,1936(A. Duncan) SWIFT of 1911 (below) was built at Leith by Ramage & Ferguson, and was sold in 1929 to the Aberdeen Steam Navigation Co. Ltd and renamed HARLAW. After a long career under the Chinese flag she arrived at Hong Kong in August,1963 for breaking up.

withdrawn at the end of the 1911 service, and sold the following year to Tripcovich & Company for Venice to Trieste service.

However in the opening year of the new century trade was again damaged by a strike of labourers and lightermen. In 1902 the company was financially reconstructed and registered under the Companies Acts, and two changes were made at the highest level to the Board of directors. Richard White was made Chairman and Managing Director, having been a director for ten years, and Capt. H. B. Hooper was made Vice-Chairman and joint Managing Director. Company secretary at this time was Charles H. Glyn, having been appointed in 1883 and he also joined the Board in 1910. Some interesting very small coasters joined the company at this time, including the new Tyne-built coaster *Pearl* of 191 grt in 1901, the new sisters *Bullfinch* and *Goldfinch* of 246 grt from Selby in 1903, the old Leith-built coaster *Jeanie Hope* of 105 grt dating from 1881, and *Kelvinside* of 219 grt built back in 1893 by Scott of Bowling as *Hare*.

The Mediterranean trader *Cygnet* was lost by fire in the Bay of Biscay in December, 1903 while outward bound to the Mediterranean carrying a mixed cargo of coal, 57 casks of binoxide of barium, old rope, 380 bags of ammonia, 80 casks of tallow, 81 casks of seed oil, 15 barrels of oil, 700 bags of manure, scrap iron nails and general cargo. The total manifest was 2,000 tons with the binoxide of barium contained in oak casks, hooped with iron and lined with glazed calico and paper. The subsequent Court of Enquiry was unable to determine the exact cause of the fire in this very explosive mixture of cargoes. She was replaced by two new Mediterranean traders of 2030 grt, the sisters *Stork* and *Crane* of 1904 built by Ropner of Stockton.

In 1906 the company acquired **John Crisp & Son** of Lowestoft with a service to London and river service to Norwich. Thus several Norfolk wherries came into the company's possession, which were too small to include in the company's now revived fleet of 55 coasters. An East Anglian shipping subsidiary, the Great Yarmouth Shipping Co. Ltd, was formed during the inter-war years to continue these services from East Anglian ports and Goole. In 1909 the company purchased the freehold of Brewers, Chesters and Galley Quays which they had long been using. In the same year the company moved to brand new offices at 15 Trinity Square opposite the Tower of London.

On the 28th December, 1908 an earthquake and tidal wave demolished the port of Messina on Sicily, completely wrecking all buildings and the magnificent quay of around one mile in length and 300 feet wide. All buildings

Tower Bridge London

LEEUWARDEN of 1903 sailing from the Pool of London to Holland (above) and at sea (below) was built by Sir Raylton Dixon & Co. Ltd on Teesside. She became a war loss on 17th March,1915.

facing the quay were destroyed with masonry sent crashing onto the heads of the local population. The company's *Drake* was hit by the two shock waves and she was thrown by the tidal wave broadside onto the quay, heeling over to an angle of 45 degrees. When thrown back into the flood she collided with one Italian and one Norwegian ship, and all three were then lashed together at anchor for safety. The beautiful city of Messina had been completely destroyed up to its famous cliffs and thousands of people killed. The crew of *Drake* provided humanitarian relief to the survivors, before sailing 24 hours later to the relative safety of Syracuse harbour, 70 miles away. She disembarked some 317 refugees including many injured, with the ship's smoking room turned into a hospital and all cabins given up to those in need. One young English lady was also saved from the holocaust at Messina and she worked tirelessly to nurse the injured. *Drake* sailed on to Milazzo and Palermo, and after returning home, Capt. Carter and his gallant crew were presented with a Gold Medal from the Italian ambassador in London.

On 16th January,1913 the Lamport & Holt passenger ship *Veronese* of 7877 grt, built by Workman, Clark & Co. Ltd at Belfast in 1906, was wrecked near Leixoes in Portugal while on a voyage from the Mersey to the Plate. General Steam's *Balgownie* was lying in Oporto at the time a few miles to the south. Capt. J. Goodson, second mate J. R. Dicks and steward A. Tingey were able to get the first rockets to the ship from shore and a hawser was passed to the stricken ship. The first people landed were eight women but the line parted and after searching Leixoes some new block and tackle and 2.5" manilla ropes were found and the line reconnected. Altogether over one hundred people including all of the passengers were saved by breeches buoy, and the rest of the crew were taken off by the Leixoes lifeboat. The Admiralty sent expressions of appreciation of good work done by Capt. Goodson and his crew.

The fleet had been augmented during this period by further large well-deckers for the Bordeaux service from London and Southampton. *Ortolan* of 1917 grt in 1902 and *Grive* of 2037 grt in 1905, both from the famous Caledon yard at Dundee, were broadly developments of *Hirondelle* of 1890 but with an extra deck amidships to give a considerable passenger carrying capacity. They made occasional voyages off-route to the Mediterranean, for which the sisters *Crane* and *Stork* of 2030 grt built in 1904 by the Ropner yard at Stockton had been specifically built. This pair were not well-deckers but ran successfully on this route for thirty years. *Drake* of 2267 grt was completed in 1908 by the Ailsa yard for the Mediterranean trades, and for a time was renamed *Wildrake* before regaining her original name and becoming a war loss in 1917. *Fauvette* of 2644 grt completed in 1912 by Sir Raylton Dixon on Teesside was a further

ORTOLAN of 1902 (above) was built by the famous Caledon yard at Dundee and was a 'well-decker'. She had considerable passenger capacity on her Bordeaux service. She became a war loss on 14th June,1917. GRIVE of 1905 (below) was a development of ORTOLAN for the Bordeaux service. She was torpedoed off Lerwick on 8th December,1917 while serving as an Armed Boarding Steamer and foundered sixteen days later. (A. Duncan)

S/S GRIVE

The General Steam Navigation Company, Ltd.

development of *Grive* and also a Bordeaux ship. As built she carried 106 passengers in one class, and all of her six lifeboats were located amidships, but later two of these were moved aft to positions on the poop, and the boat deck was shortened. Her cabins and dining saloon were on the shelter deck; bridge deck had two special cabins, a music room, smoking room and ladies' room; while the navigating bridge was placed at boat deck level. She carried a small amount of refrigerated cargo such as meat and vegetables, loaded with the help of six small deck cranes, and her triple expansion engines gave a speed of 15.34 knots on trials. She became a war loss in 1916, and a virtual repeat was then ordered from the Ailsa yard and completed in 1917 as *Philomel*. As built this ship was of 2400 grt but her tonnage openings were later closed resulting in a higher measurement of 3050 grt. She unfortunately also became a war loss in September, 1918 in a Bordeaux convoy. A new engines-aft design for a smaller vessel of 1200 grt was developed for *Corncrake* and *Laverock* of 1909/10 from the Ailsa yard for the shorter haul routes. A direct comparison was made with two engines-amidships sisters of the same size in 1911, *Lapwing* and *Swift*, with the engines aft design being favoured more consistently for this smaller size of vessel after the Great War.

THE GREAT WAR

In August,1914 the fleet stood at 46 coastal steamers of which the Admiralty requisitioned 21 company ships, subsequently releasing *Balgownie* and *Mallard*. The remaining 19 ships were employed in various duties of minelaying, minesweeping, flotilla and squadron supply, carrying ammunition and stores, fleet messages and moving troops. The company's Dockyard at Deptford was placed at the Government's disposal. Capt. H. B. Hooper, Vice-Chairman and joint Managing Director of company, served on the National Maritime Board from 1916 to 1920, dealing with the manning of ships in Government service and the scales of pay to apply to the crews of British ships. Some 17 company Masters and 18 company Chief Engineers received commissions in the Royal Naval Reserve, and a further two Masters were appointed as Intelligence Officers due to their good knowledge of Continental ports. Chairman Richard White served on the Committee of Shipowners for Mediterranean trades from 1917/19, and on the committee for trade to the Atlantic islands, Portugal and Morocco. W. J. McAlister, another director, was appointed in June,1918 as London Chairman of the Home Trade Transport Council, which organized the carriage of goods by water to relieve the pressure on the railways.

Company war losses were 18 vessels with a further five as marine losses :-

9.1914 *Auk* Interned in Germany and later sunk in the Gulf of Pernau to block the channel as defence against the Russian fleet.
9.1914 *Iris* Interned in Germany and later sunk in the Gulf of Pernau to block the channel as defence against the German fleet.
22.10.1914 *Adjutant* Sunk by collision in The Downs off Deal o.v. Naples to London with general cargo.
30.1.1915 *Oriole* Torpedoed/sunk by U20 in English Channel o.v. London to Havre with general cargo. 21 lost including the Master.

DRAKE of 1908 (above) was built by the yard that built more ships than any other for the company - the Ailsa yard at Troon. She served on the Bordeaux and Mediterranean routes and became a war loss on 30th September,1917. SEAMEW of 1915 (below) was also built at Troon and was sold for further service in 1938, being broken up at Dublin in 1953.

17.3.1915 *Leeuwarden* Captured/sunk by gunfire in North Sea 4m W by N1/2N from Maas L. V. by U28 o.v. London to Harlingen in ballast.
15.4.1915 *Ptarmigan* Torpedoed/sunk in North Sea 6 m NW of North Hinder L. V. by UB5 o.v. Rotterdam to London with general cargo. 8 lost.
23.9.1915 *Groningen* Mined/sunk off the Thames 1.5 m NE of Sunk Head buoy laid by UC6 o.v. Harlingen to London with general cargo. 1 lost.
6.2.1916 *Balgownie* Mined/sunk off the Thames 1.75m ESE of Sunk Head buoy laid by UC7 o.v. London to Leith with general cargo. 1 lost.
9.3.1916 *Fauvette* Mined/sunk in The Downs off North Foreland by UC7 o.v. Girgenti to London while on Government service as an Armed Boarding Steamer.
6.4.1916 *Vesuvio* Mined/sunk in the English Channel 6m E of Owers L.V. laid by UB29 o.v. Messina to London with general cargo. 7 lost including Master.
7.4.1916 *Halcyon* Mined/sunk in Straits of Dover 3.5m SSW of Folkestone pier laid by UC6 o.v. Bordeaux to London with general cargo.
29.4.1916 *Teal* Captured and torpedoed in North Sea 2 m E of Seaham Harbour by UB27 o.v. Leith to London.
7.7.1916 *Gannet* Mined/sunk in the North Sea 5m ENE of Shipwash L.V. laid by UC6 o.v. Rotterdam to London with general cargo. 8 lost.
8.11.1916 *Sheldrake* Captured/sunk by gunfire in the Mediterranean 20m WSW from Marittimo Island, Italy by U34 o.v. Naples to London in ballast. Master & Chief Engineer taken prisoner.
25.4.1917 *Hirondelle* Torpedoed/sunk in the Bay of Biscay 13m SE of Belle Ile by UC36 o.v. London to Bordeaux with general cargo.
14.6.1917 *Ortolan* Torpedoed/sunk 100 m WSW of Bishop Rock by U82 o.v. Genoa to London with general cargo. 3 lost.
30.9.1917 *Heron* Torpedoed/sunk in the Bay of Biscay 500m W of Belle Ile by U90 o.v. Tyne to Oporto with coal. 22 lost including Master.
30.9.1917 *Drake* Captured/sunk by gunfire 340 m W of Ushant by U90 o.v. London to Genoa with general cargo & explosives. Master taken prisoner.
11.11.1917 *Lapwing* Mined/sunk in the North Sea 9m SE of Southwold by UC4 o.v. Rotterdam to London with general cargo.
8.12.1917 *Grive* Torpedoed in the North Sea off Lerwick by UC40 while on Government service as an Armed Boarding Steamer, sank 16 days later.
29.12.1917 *Peregrine* Wrecked near Sunk L.V. o.v. Rotterdam to Harwich, all crew & 39 passengers rescued.
7.3.1918 *Starling* Collision/sunk 7 miles W of Treport o.v. London to Bordeaux.
16.9.1918 *Philomel* Torpedoed/sunk in the Bay of Biscay 12m ESE of Iles de Glenan near Lorient by UB88 o.v. London to Brest and Bordeaux with general cargo.

On the outbreak of war, *Alouette* was the last ship out of Ostend on 21st August, and *Laverock* was the last ship out of Zeebrugge the next day, with *Gannet* later the last ship out of Antwerp. *Auk* (Capt. Hughes), *Iris* (Capt. Ford) and *Virgo* (Capt. Finney) were detained at Cuxhaven and sent to Brunsbuttel on 3rd August. They repeatedly tried to get back to sea but were turned back. Capt. Hughes was returned home during 1917 and Capt. Finney returned during March,1918, but Capt. Ford was in captivity for the whole of the war. *Auk* and *Iris* were both later sunk in the Gulf of Pernau to block the channel as defence against the Russian fleet. *Redstart* and *Nautilus* (renamed *Nautpur*) served as guardships at Harwich throughout the war. Many of the company ships did sterling war service as troopships, with *Lapwing* among the first ships to carry troops from Southampton to France, and excursion ship *Golden Eagle* used as a troopship from Southampton throughout the war, during which she carried no fewer than 518,101 troops, and was later converted into a seaplane carrier.

Fauvette was in Bordeaux when war was declared, and brought back 144 British subjects to London, then trooped from Southampton to Rouen before being employed as a despatch vessel at Bordeaux, the seat of the French Goverment for the majority of the war. In March 1915 she took the boom defence for Mudros in the Aegean Sea and laid it, and was then commissioned as an Armed Boarding Vessel, searching for submarines and escorting troopships for the Dardanelles. She carried troops to Suvla Bay and cruised off the Bulgarian coast to embark refugees from the Serbian Army for Corfu. As detailed above she was sunk in the English Channel on 9th March,1916 after leaving Greek waters in February,1916.

Heron and *Drake* were lost on the same outward convoy to the Mediterranean on 30th September,1917. They were three days out from Falmouth in company with a convoy of nearly thirty ships, whose escort had left them the previous evening. *Heron* was struck by a torpedo in the engine room at 1 a.m. and quickly sank, claiming the lives of twenty crew including the Master, with one person picked up by the attacking submarine U90. *Drake* was shelled and sunk at 10 a.m. by the same U-boat and quickly blew up as she was carrying explosives and general cargo. Capt. Carter was taken prisoner on the U-boat, and the rest of the crew took to the boats and were picked up twelve hours later by the *Cronstadt* (Capt. Logan) who had fought the same submarine for two hours after the destruction of *Drake* and had escaped behind a smokescreen.

On 11th November, 1917 *Lapwing* under Capt. W.G. Branthwaite was mined and sunk nine miles to SE of Southwold while on a voyage from Rotterdam to London with general cargo. Her Master was stunned by the explosion and was buried under the wreckage of the fore hatch but managed to escape in a lifeboat, the hatches of the sinking ship blowing up as it pushed off. All of the crew were picked up by the destroyer *Surprise*. The brand new *Philomel* under Commore Wilson was torpedoed and sunk in the Bay of Biscay as the last company vessel lost on 16th September, 1918. She was by far the most valuable ship in the convoy, but was foolishly placed at the head of the convoy and on its flank by the naval authorities. Her Master, officers and crew were rescued by the United States Navy patrol ship *Rambler*.

A sequel to the seizing of *Virgo* at Cuxhaven at the beginning of the war occurred after the war had ended. She had been interned at Brunsbuttel for the duration of the war and the crew sent to Internment Camp, where Chief Engineer Alfred Cockle was given a medical innoculation with vicious force into his tatooed right arm. After the war, *Virgo* continued on the Hamburg service and one day a member of her crew fell ill and a doctor was sent for. The doctor who arrived was none other than the one from the Internment Camp, and Chief Engineer Cockle accelerated his departure after a very short stay on the ship with the same force as he had received during the war. Also sharing the same internment camp was the Hamburg manager, Percy Privitt, later the secretary and a director of the company, and a man destined to rise to the position of Chairman, Robert Kelso.

INTER - WAR YEARS

At the end of the war a large rebuilding programme was begun, with orders for ten new ships of around 1500 grt for the main Continental routes with six orders for the favoured Ailsa yard at Troon, and a further 14 coasters of up to 500 grt were either built new for the company or were purchased by 1925. Five of the larger class *Lapwing, Petrel, Auk, Teal* and *Gannet* were of a new engines-aft design, pioneered by the sisters *Laverock* and *Corncrake* of 1909, which were the first newbuildings for the company from the Ailsa yard. The other five larger newbuildings were to the more traditional engines-amidships design and named *Heron, Starling, Halcyon, Philomel* and *Drake*. The engines-aft sisters were used on the services to Fecamp to the north of Le Havre, Antwerp, and Hamburg; and the engines amidships sisters on the Bordeaux, Lisbon and occasional Mediterranean trading. Three of the small 500 grt coasters came from the Newcastle coaster fleets of G.T. Gillie & Blair Ltd with *Pentland Firth, Beauly Firth* and *Glanton Firth* being renamed *Alouette, Ortolan*, and *Ptarmigan* respectively. Two larger ships of nearly 2000 grt were purchased second-hand for regular Mediterranean trading, with the elder of the pair dating from 1909 coming from Far Eastern owners to be renamed *Guillemot*, and the almost new *Myrtlepark* coming from J. & J. Denholm Ltd of Glasgow to be renamed *Adjutant*. A sister of the latter was completed by the same shipbuilder for the company in 1924 and named *Albatross*.

In 1919 the company branch offices in Germany (3), Holland (3), France (4) and one in Italy were re-opened after the war. Also in that year the company purchased the trade and goodwill of the Humber - London service of G. R. Haller Ltd, and also the London - Ghent service of Leach & Company. In September of that year *Falcon* made the first voyage to Hamburg from London since 1914. The company at this time owned two quays near to Tower Bridge - Brewer's Quay (including Chester's Quay and Galley Quay); and Irongate and St. Katharine's Wharf. The company also used loading and

STARLING of 1920 is seen as BALTALLIN (above) of United Baltic Shipping Co. Ltd, to whom she was sold in 1930. She became a war loss on 20th September,1941. Her sister HERON of 1920 (below) was also sold to United Baltic in 1935 to become BALTEAKO, and sank after striking a mine in Kiel Bay on 29th March,1946.

LAPWING of 1920 (above)was built by Bow, McLachlan on the Clyde and served the company until she became a war loss on 26th September,1941 while returning in convoy from Gibraltar, her sister PETREL being lost in the same convoy. GANNET of 1921 (below) from the same builder survived the war and sailed on for the company until December,1953 when she arrived at Grays in Essex for breaking up. (F.R. Sherlock)

discharging berths at the north, south and east quays in the P.L.A. London Dock at Wapping, and on the south side of the river at Butler's Wharf, and on the north side above Tower Bridge at Fresh Wharf, immediately below London Bridge. One or two ships were discharged each day by lighters while moored at tiers in the river. The loading/discharging location for each of the company's main trades was :-

HAMBURG	- Butler's Wharves, the only quays used on the south side of the river..
BORDEAUX	- British & Foreign Wharf
LEITH/GHENT	- Irongate & St. Katherine's Wharf
MEDITERRANEAN	- Fresh Wharf/Nicholson's Wharf
AMSTERDAM/ HARLINGEN	- Brewers Quay next to Tower Hill
ROTTERDAM	- Carron Wharf
N. FRENCH PORTS	- St. Katherine's Dock
HULL	- St. Katherine's Wharf
TONNAY CHARENTE & OPORTO	- Wapping P.L.A. Dock

In 1920 the payroll included some 880 sea-going staff, sixty office staff, with up to 450 casual dockers/lumpers employed at St. Katharine's Wharf and Dock, and more than 500 casual dockers/lumpers at Brewer's Quay. Company fleet strength in 1920 was 32 ships, and later that year the company was taken over by the **P. & O. Steam Navigation Co. Ltd.** As with nearly all of their acquisitions no internal changes were made to the company until 1936, when one of their directors began to sit on the Board. The transaction was actually made via Gray, Dawes & Company, P. & O.'s agency in the Persian Gulf owned by Lord Inchcape and was passed to the parent company at cost price. The deep-sea liner company's European position was much strengthened by the acquisition of the company's many Continental agencies. Viscount Inchcape and Viscount Chelmsford acted as trustees for the new debenture holders. The initial post-war optimism was reflected in the good company dividends of 15% for 1919 and 1920. However company dividends slumped to only 5% from 1921 to 1925, when the coaster fleet had recovered to 48 ships of 46,838 grt, not including the company's two excursion ships *Eagle*, built in 1898, and *Golden Eagle*, built in 1909, for the summer Thames excursion trade to Southend, Herne Bay, Clacton, Ramsgate and Margate.

Rationalisation of competing services with other coasting lines began to appear in the 1920s due to the anticipated levels of trade not being met. In

ALOUETTE of 1920 (above) was purchased in 1924 as PENTLAND FIRTH from G.T. Gillie & Blair of Newcastle. She was sunk at Normandy on 22nd June,1944. ORTOLAN of 1920 was purchased in 1923 as BEAULY FIRTH from the same Newcastle owners. She is seen as BANNTRADER (below) of W. Coe to whom she was sold in 1950, and she arrived for scrap at Preston in August,1962.

PETREL of 1920 is seen moored in the Thames with her sister TEAL behind her (above). She was sunk returning in a Gibraltar convoy on 26th September,1941 along with her sister LAPWING. (A. Duncan) FAUVETTE of 1925 (below) was built by J. Samuel White & Co. Ltd at Cowes and was sunk in collision in the North Sea on 25th October,1934 while on a voyage from Antwerp to London. (A. Duncan)

1923 a new company, the **Great Yarmouth Shipping Co. Ltd**, was formed jointly with T. Small & Co.(Great Yarmouth) Ltd to operate services between London and Great Yarmouth via Lowestoft, and Yarmouth and Hull, and several Norfolk wherries came into the possession of the company for trading on the Norfolk Broads to Norwich. This new company then in 1931 took over General Steam's warehouses, wharves and river services at Great Yarmouth, Lowestoft and Norwich as well as the T. Small shipbroking business at Great Yarmouth. The new company's fleet was only two old coasters dating from as far back as 1903 until General Steam transferred four of its fleet, *Goldfinch, Peronne, Picardy* and *Yellowhammer*, to it during the Depression years. The familiar nomenclature of East Anglian and Lincolnshire towns followed by the word *'Trader'* also started towards the end of the Depression years with two old steam coasters, *Norwich Trader* built in 1908 at Selby by Cochrane & Sons and *Yarmouth Trader* built in the town of its name by Crabtree & Co. Ltd in 1920. Two motor coasters of 380 grt were then completed in 1934 and 1936 as *Lowestoft Trader* and *Boston Trader* by Goole Shipbuilding & Engineering Co. Ltd with 6-cylinder diesels by British Auxiliaries Ltd of Glasgow. General Steam continued to transfer ships to the new company in post-war years, whose funnel colours were yellow with a black top.

The Vice-Chairman of the company, Capt. H. B. Hooper, had died in 1923 and was replaced by W. J. McAlister, who had joined the Board in 1914 from Clan Line. The other two directors were then Richard White, Chairman, and Charles H. Glyn, the former secretary, who died shortly after his retirement in 1924. Richard White's death in 1926 was a another great blow to the company in 1926, and their replacements on the Board were Robert Kelso and Stanley Sparkes, with W. J. McAlister then promoted to Chairman, a post he held until his death in 1937 when Robert Kelso took over the helm of the company.

During the General Strike of 1926, office staff from the Trinity Square headquarters helped unload company vessels at the nearby company wharves. In 1927 General Steam expanded by taking over from Ellerman Wilson Line their service between London and Bremen, which added another link to its chain of connections with the Continent. In 1931 the **Rhine - London Line** was taken over, and marked the start of their well-remembered Rhine ports service run with the company's smallest ships for the next forty years. In 1933 the interests in the **London & Dunkirk Shipping Company**, formerly jointly owned by the company and the **Bennett Steamship Co. Ltd** of Goole were taken over. The latter company's service to Boulogne and Calais was also taken over, reviving a very old connection between General Steam and

CRESTED EAGLE was built in 1925 by J. Samuel White & Co. Ltd at Cowes. She became a war loss at Dunkirk on 29th May,1940 (From a painting by Jack Spurling). ROYAL EAGLE was built in 1932 by Cammell,Laird & Co. Ltd at Birkenhead and is seen approaching Tilbury Pier on 19th August,1933. She was broken up in 1954. (Pamlin Prints)

FALCON of 1927 (above) was completed by the Ailsa yard and uniquely had her navigating bridge positioned forwards. Also note her four General Steam Patent electric cranes, a feature of many of the company's ships built after 1920. She arrived at Bo'ness for breaking up in March,1957. (F.R. Sherlock) ADJUTANT of 1921 (below) was completed at Grangemouth as MYRTLEPARK for J. & J. Denholm of Glasgow and was purchased and renamed in 1924. She ran to the Mediterranean and was sold to British owners in 1950, eventually stranding off Istria on 27th February,1964 and was refloated and broken up at Trieste shortly after. She had an identical sister ALBATROSS built in 1924 for the company by the same yard.

Boulogne after a period of 45 years. The remaining trades and goodwill of the Bennett Steamship Co. Ltd were fully acquired in 1946.

The company's Thames excursion trade received a boost in 1925 with the delivery by J. Samuel White & Co. Ltd of Cowes of *Crested Eagle* of 1110 grt, powered by oil-fired triple expansion engines to give a speed of 18.5 knots. She was commanded by Capt. F.G. Cole from delivery until his retirement in 1939, having joined the company in 1899, becoming Chief Officer in 1902, Master in 1910 and who served in the Harlingen trades in the winter months. She originally ran from Old Swan Pier before Tower Pier was built, and often found herself in competition with *Royal Sovereign* of 1893 until the latter was purchased from Palace Steamers in 1929. *Royal Sovereign* was considered to be the fastest excursion steamer on the river and flew a cock at her masthead. On one occasion *Crested Eagle* beat her to Margate, and on the following day a cock was flown from her masthead. Next morning a parcel was delivered while Capt. Cole was having breakfast which on opening was found to be a large quantity of bird-seed, spreading all over the breakfast table much to the annoyance of Capt. Cole. A note accompanied with the compliments of Palace Steamers !

The company's last new paddle steamer for this trade was delivered by Cammell, Laird & Co. Ltd at Birkenhead in 1932 as *Royal Eagle* of 1532 grt with oil-burning 3-cylinder steam reciprocating engine to give a service speed of 17.5 knots. She was the ultimate in the long development of the paddle steamer in terms of manoeuvrability, beauty and large deck passenger capacity for some 2,000 passengers. *Crested Eagle* was switched to the new service to Clacton and Felixstowe at the beginning of the 1932 season, with *Royal Eagle* and *Golden Eagle* serving Margate and Ramsgate, the old *Eagle* of 1898 having gone for scrap in 1928. The sailing schedule in the 1930s was much the same as it was at the turn of the century, with one paddle steamer picking up passengers at four river points for Southend, Margate and Ramsgate, while the other operated a direct service to Margate and Ramsgate from London Bridge. *Golden Eagle* under Capt. Branthwaite usually operated this latter service, leaving her enough time to run a short sea cruise from Margate from 1445 to 1630 hours, giving Margate holidaymakers a trip around the Kentish Knock Lightship and back around the south buoy to port ready to pick up her day trippers for return to London Bridge. There was even an upmarket air service from Croydon Airport for well-heeled passengers by Hillman's Airways Ltd to join the return leg of her sea and river cruise at Ramsgate, with the GSNC logo proudly painted on the fuselage of the biplane.

HIRONDELLE of 1925 (above) was built by Greenock Dockyard and survived World War II. She transferred to the Moss-Hutchison fleet in 1948 as LANDES and was sold to Italian owners in 1953 and broken up at Lubeck in June,1961 after a stranding in the Gulf of Bothnia. ROEK of 1925 (below) from the same Ailsa yard became a war loss on 12th May,1940.

WOODCOCK of 1927 (above) was built at Grangemouth for the regular London to Leith route, where she was also registered. She transferred to the Moss-Hutchison fleet in 1939 and renamed a LORMONT and was sunk by collision off the Humber on 7th December,1940 while acting as a guard ship. (A. Duncan) CORMORANT of 1927 (below) was built by Earle's of Hull and had a thirty year career with the company until she arrived at Grays in Essex for scrap on 27th June,1957.

The company fleet strength in 1930 stood at 45 ships, of which six were new engines amidships vessels of around 1500 grt for the Continental routes. All but one, *Cormorant*, had been built by the favoured Ailsa yard at Troon which delivered her near sisters *Falcon*, *Woodlark*, *Starling*, *Groningen* and *Leeuwarden* during a three year period from 1927. The previous *Starling* of 1920 was sold in 1930 to the United Baltic Steamship Co. Ltd, which also purchased her sister *Heron* in 1935. The terms of a joint service with W. H. Muller was the reason for the Dutch names of two of the newbuildings and used on the Rotterdam service, as had the previous pair with the same names dating from 1902/3. This new sextet were very successful for the company with only one war loss, *Leeuwarden*, and all of the others gave 30 years of service, with *Starling* of 1930 lasting until the end of 1960 before arriving at Grays, Essex for scrap while *Groningen* of 1928 lasted until the middle of 1961 before arriving at the same scrapyard although renamed as *Philomel* for her last three years of service. The Leith route obtained a new trader in 1927, *Woodcock* of 1827 grt, joining the fleet from the nearby Grangemouth yard. Two smaller coasters, *Mavis* and *Swift*, joined from the Belfast yard of Workman,Clark & Co. Ltd in 1930 and were placed on the Antwerp route, and were of the same size as the *Roek*, *Merel*, *Fauvette*, *Hirondelle* and *Grebe* of 1925/26.

The company carried the vast majority of both the port wine and brandy imports into England on the 14-day service from Tonnay Charente. The new *Grebe* of 1926 carried 28,000 cases of brandy home from there in December,1927 - a record for the company with some of the cargo destined to be transshipped for Far Eastern countries. *Philomel* and *Halcyon* were sisters of 1570 grt built by the Ailsa yard in 1920/21 and carried 12 passengers on the Bordeaux run at a service speed of 12 knots on their 14-day service. Their wood-sheathed top decks were particularly easy for the crew to keep clean. A strike of cranemen in the summer of 1928 at Quai-des-Chartrons near the Pont de Pierre at Bordeaux resulted in the crew of *Philomel* using her G.S.N. Patent electric cranes to discharge some 200 tons of empty wine casks and waste paper bales. Working in two gangs of six from Monday to Saturday, a full cargo of wine was then loaded for the homeward voyage as follows :-

No. 1 Hold - Chestnut extract casks and wine cases
No. 2 Main Hold - Two tiers of resin casks below five tiers of wine cases, blocked off with cases of mushrooms.
No. 3 Hold - Wine cases and general cargo.
'Tween decks - Cases of wine and shelled walnuts, and light bundles of hoop sticks and straw.

GRONINGEN was built in 1928 by the Ailsa yard and renamed PHILOMEL by the company in 1958 as seen above (A. Duncan). She is seen below after collision on 26th April,1961 and she was beached at Gravesend Reach. She was refloated the next day and taken to Grays in Essex for breaking up. (J. Clarkson)

WIFT of 1930 is seen in Moss-Hutchison colours. She was renamed LORMONT in 1948 and ld in 1953 and broken up at Hong Kong in 1968. WOODLARK of 1928 (below) is also seen in oss-Hutchison colours, and was sold for further trading in 1954 and broken up in India in 1967.

The cranemen's strike was over a week later when her sister *Halcyon* arrived to load. The company served the following main ports in the inter-war years :-

NORTH EUROPEAN SERVICES FROM LONDON

Amsterdam, Antwerp, Bordeaux, Boulogne, Bremen, Calais, Charente, Dunkirk, Leith, Ghent, Hamburg, Harlingen, Harwich, Havre, Hull, Lowestoft, Lisbon, Middlesbrough, Newcastle, Newlyn, Oporto, Ostend, Rhine ports, Rotterdam, Southampton, Terneuzen and Great Yarmouth.

MEDITERRANEAN SERVICES FROM LONDON

Malaga & Valencia in Spain
Bastia in Corsica
Algiers & Oran in North Africa
12 ports in Italy:- Genoa, Catania, Civitavecchia, Livorno,
Marsala, Messina, Naples, Palermo, Pozzuoli, Savona, Spezia, Syracuse.
Patras & Piraeus in Greece
Izmir & Istanbul in Turkey

The doyen of the fleet, *Tern* of 1875 under Capt. Herbert, was lost following a collision in March, 1931 in the Humber, having given 56 years of service to the company. The first motor vessel in the fleet was the Dutch-built *Tern* of 1932, which was used in the home trades to see if it possessed its claimed advantages of speed and reliability over the steamship. The results were very good, and in 1934 an order was placed with the Haverton Hill yard of Furness Shipbuilding on the Tees for a motorship of 614 grt costing £33,000 and completed as *Fauvette*. She replaced a steamer of the same name lost by collision in the North Sea on 25th October, 1934 while on a voyage from Amsterdam to London. Dividends during the Depression years were kept at 5%, only slightly below the 6% dividends paid between 1926 and 1930.

A staff pension scheme was introduced in the company in 1933 which was soon extended to masters, officers and engineers of all of the company's ships. Several seafarers of the time had justifiably earned their pension, with Commodore H. Wilson having 55 years service on retirement in 1927, Commodore Carter having 50 years service on retirement in 1934, Capt. Wills having more than 60 years service when he retired as Marine Superintendent in 1929, having held the post since 1898. The latter was succeeded by Capt.

'ERN of 1932 was the company's first motorship when built in Holland by J. Koster. She was old in 1949 and is seen as GEORGE EMELIE above, and after a long career of 57 years was cuttled in March,1989. (A. Duncan) CRANE of 1937 is seen in Moss-Hutchison colours (below). he was sold in 1964 and broken up at Kuwait in 1982 (A. Duncan)

PHILOMEL of 1936 is seen sailing from Grand harbour, Valletta in Malta. She was built by th famous Caledon yard at Dundee and after distinguished war service and post-war service with th company was sold to Italian owners in 1957. She became a total loss when she ran aground 15 miles East of Lagos on 15th February,1967. Her motor-driven near sister HERON of 1937 (below) was also from the Caledon yard and also had a distinguished war record. She transferre to Moss-Hutchison in 1956 to become KUFRA, and was sold in 1959 and broken up at Split in September,1974 (A. Duncan)

Spearpoint, and in turn by Capt. A. H. Hutton in 1935, who had joined the company in 1920 as 2nd Mate of *Alouette* on the Ostend run. He became Mate in 1921, Master in 1926 commanding in turn *Laverock, Corncrake, Tern, Fauvette, Hirondelle, Starling* and *Guillemot*. He was later awarded an OBE 'in recognition of services rendered to the national effort during the war'. Willoughby K. John, secretary of the company, retired in 1934 after 49 years of service, 24 as secretary.

The company's Mediterranean traders during the Depression were the elderly *Stork* of 1904, her sister *Crane* having been sold to Yugoslavian owners in 1930, *Adjutant* of 1922 and her sister *Albatross* of 1924, *Drake* of 1922 which also was used on the Bordeaux wine run. The Mediterranean trades were ripe for rationalisation and this took place at the end of the Great Depression on 17th October,1934, when the company acquired the business and fleet of the **Moss Hutchison Line** of Liverpool for £388,859. This company had only been formed six months earlier by the merger on 6th April,1934 of J. & P. Hutchison of Glasgow (formed 1860) and the old-established Moss Line of Liverpool (1823) to give a 22-ship fleet. Hutchison was a Royal Mail Group member and this merger was part of the liquidation efforts of Royal Mail. The Moss Line trade was from Liverpool/Glasgow to Bordeaux, the Eastern Mediterranean, the Black Sea and occasionally to Mauritius for sugar. The Hutchison trade was Dublin and West Coast U. K. ports as well as Hamburg/Bremen/Rouen to Bordeaux and Portugal and Spain, returning with wine and brandy. Moss - Hutchison Line retained its own offices and management in co-operation with General Steam's Mediterranean services after the take-over. This was by far the most important of 30 subsidiaries, mostly land-based, owned by General Steam, and an appendix at the rear of this book details the fleet which numbered 16 vessels at the beginning of 1935 on take-over.

At the end of the Depression the General Steam fleet consisted of forty owned vessels, not including those of Moss - Hutchison Line, and was boosted by two large new Mediterranean traders in the steamer *Philomel* from the Caledon yard in 1936 and her slightly larger motor-driven sister *Heron* of 1937 from the same yard, and fitted with portable decks in her holds. *Philomel* and *Heron* introduced new paint schemes for the fleet with the previous brown upperworks and bridge structures now painted white and the black funnel now sporting the addition of the company houseflag. Hull colour remained black with a white line, and after the war from 1947 the new colour scheme became standard for all of the fleet, which were repainted as overhauls became due. The small electric deck cranes, which were such a feature of all of the

FAUVETTE of 1935 was built by the Furness yard on Teesside and served the company for nearly thirty years. She was sold for further trading and was used at the end of her career to supply Grand Cayman Island in the Caribbean with supplies as ISLAND SUPPLIER. (A. Duncan) GOLDFINCH of 1937 from the Caledon yard was sold in 1962 and eventually broken up at Eleusis in Greece in December,1984 (A. Duncan)

PLOVER of 1936 from the Caledon yard transferred to the Great Yarmouth Shipping Co. Ltd in 1960, shortly before her collision and sinking in the New Waterway on 7th November,1961 (A. Duncan) DRAKE of 1938 (below) was built to a 'New Koster' engines amidships design in Holland. She was sold in 1966 and deleted from the register in 1991.

company's new ships built after 1920, and masts remained as brown. In 1936 two small motor vessels, *Mallard* and *Plover*, of 352 grt, were completed at the Caledon yard at Dundee for the trade to Northern French ports, and four further larger motorships were completed within a year as *Bullfinch*, *Goldfinch*, *Crane* and *Stork* with service speeds of between 10 and 11 knots.

At the end of 1936 the company acquired the **New Medway Steam Packet Co. Ltd** of Rochester and thus virtually controlled the entire Thames summer excursion trade. The take-over occurred in the centenary year of the New Medway company, whose most famous member of its fleet of eight excursion vessels was the former Mersey ferry *Daffodil*, which had played such a heroic part at Zeebrugge in the Great War that she was given a 'Royal' prefix to her name. The newest member was the Denny-built *Queen of the Channel* of 1935 and these two pleasure fleets in 1936 were composed of the following vessels :-

GENERAL STEAM	**NEW MEDWAY S.P.**
Golden Eagle of 1909	Essex Queen of 1897
Crested Eagle of 1925	Medway Queen of 1924
Royal Eagle of 1932	Queen of Kent of 1916
Isle of Arran of 1892	Queen of Southend of 1898
Laguna Belle of 1896	Queen of Thanet of 1916
	Queen of the Channel of 1935
	Royal Daffodil of 1906
	City of Rochester of 1904

The company had been using the title **Eagle Steamers Ltd** since 1932 for its own Thames-based excursions, and the Medway-based excursions of their new acquisition, commonly known as the **Queen Line of Steamers of Rochester,** were seen as complementary to their own excursions as each company drew their customers from different starting points on the run to Margate and Ramsgate. The new excursion vessels built in 1937 and 1939, *Royal Sovereign* and *Royal Daffodil*, had twin propellers with extended side sponsons, and enabled the company to carry out a pre-war programme of Cross-Channel excursions. The new *Royal Sovereign* was a motorship and an enlarged repeat of *Queen of the Channel*, which had been the first diesel-driven excursion ship on the Thames. *Royal Daffodil* was a twin-funnelled motorship and happily survived the war. General Steam's empire of coastal ships could now rightly claim to have ships with *'Royal'* names in their fleet. The company

ORIOLE of 1939 (above) was built at Leith by the Henry Robb yard. She was sold to Canadian owners in 1962, and after a long career sank off Santo Domingo Cay in the Bahamas on New Years Day, 1991 while on a voyage from Miami to Gonaives in Haiti. (A. Duncan)
MALLARD was built in 1938 in Holland by Smit & Zoon as WEST COASTER for the British Isles Coasters Ltd. She was purchased by the company in 1943 and renamed MALLARD in 1950. She was broken up at Gravesend in September,1984 after a second career as a dredger.

The twin-funnelled QUEEN of the CHANNEL excursion ship was built in 1935 by the Denny yard and became a war loss during the Dunkirk evacuation on 28th May,1940. Her larger fleetmate ROYAL DAFFODIL (below) was built in 1939 by Denny and served during the war for the Admiralty and for the company until withdrawn from excursion service in 1966. She arrived at Ghent for scrap on 1st February,1967 (Company).

now had a monopoly of the Thames excursion trade, and with war approaching passenger numbers rose sharply during the 1938 and 1939 seasons as people were determined to enjoy themselves before the threat of war became a reality.

General Steam formed a new subsidiary at the end of the Depression for the Antwerp and Rotterdam liner services from London in **Grand Union Shipping Co. Ltd** with offices in the Port of London Building in Seething Lane and not at their Trinity Square headquarters. A Dutch coaster was purchased in 1937 for the new company and was renamed *Marsworth*, the suffix *'Worth'* subsequently being used for all of their ships. She had been built in 1925 by J. Smit at Vierverlaten as *Koningsdiep* and was purchased as *Merwede*. She was continued in service after the war until sold in 1949 for further service.

Three new engines-amidships motorships were delivered in 1938 from the Koster yard in Holland to their 'New Koster' design. *Drake* of 531 grt and the smaller pair of *Alouette* and *Kingfisher* of 278 grt were shelterdeckers and ideal for the company's Rhine ports trades. In 1939 an interest was acquired in **Turner, Edwards & Co. Ltd** of Bristol and their Edwards Bristol Channel Lines Ltd, and was later completely taken over. During the inter-war years the number of Continental agencies had greatly increased, representing many British and Continental shipping lines, and the company fleet in 1939 stood at 36 vessels including 12 motor vessels. A 7.5% dividend was paid on ordinary and preference shares in 1937, however company trading results in 1938 were 200,000 tons down on 1937, reflecting the fact that European trade with Britain during the last ten years had dropped from 33% of total British trade to only 26.3%, a trend that was to continue after the coming destruction of war.

WORLD WAR II

The company fleet and all of its seafarers now began the serious business of avoiding bombs, torpedoes and mines as well as coping with the usually excruciatingly boring patrols and maintaining station in the large convoys of the next six years. Seven of the company's excursion steamers were deployed during the first three days of September,1939 in taking children from the capital as evacuees to Felixstowe, Lowestoft and Yarmouth. Some 19,578 children began new wartime lives, and all of these excursion steamers were subsequently engaged in transporting the troops of the British Expeditionary Force to France. However their greatest test under heavy aerial and shore bombardment came during the withdrawal of this force from Dunkirk during 26th May to 4th June,1940. The individual exploits of these shallow-draft craft and the smaller cargo ships are now given :-

Golden Eagle made at least three trips to Dunkirk, bringing back over 2,000 troops. Her first trip had to be aborted when she rescued the troops and crew of the sinking paddle steamer *Waverley* and returned to Margate with them. On her second trip she was in the area of Dunkirk East pier for all of the daylight hours of one day, with men being rescued from the beach by her lifeboats. The pier was used at night for embarkation, since a stationary ship at the pier during daylight was risky and would soon be sunk by the enemy. Her last trip in the final days of the evacuation was at night.

Crested Eagle arrived at Dunkirk at 1400 hours on 29th May and berthed alongside the East pier. German planes successively destroyed a trawler, a cross-Channel passenger ship and a destroyer, with troops transferring from one ship to another and finally to board *Crested Eagle*. As she left harbour, two aerial bombs struck her in the engine room and stern and set her on fire. She was beached further along the coast and became a total loss.

KINGFISHER of 1944 was the first British coaster to provide single cabins for all of her ratings. She was sold in 1966 to Canadian owners and scuttled off St. John's (NF) in December,1983 (A.Duncan) STORK of 1945 (below) was built by the Henry Robb yard at Leith and sold to Greek owners in 1966. She is still in service today in Greek waters.

Royal Eagle made three rescue trips, the first two from La Panne during the daylight hours of the 29th and 30th, her A.A. guns being in action all day. She left at dusk with a full complement of troops each day, being machine-gunned on the return voyage. Her final trip was to Dunkirk, evacuating troops during the night of 1st/2nd June with three boatloads of badly wounded troops taken aboard, and she left at daylight for Sheerness.

Queen of the Channel carried the Irish Guards to Boulogne for the final defence of the port. She made only one fateful trip into Dunkirk, arriving on 27th at 2000 hours. Troops were embarked at the East pier and from boats in the open roadstead, and she left at 0255 hours the next morning with 950 troops aboard. She was however attacked by a German aircraft at 0415 hours and straddled by three or four bombs which lifted her and broke her back. Capt. Odell valiantly tried to save his ship but the pumps could not contain the advance of the water, and twelve hours later all of her crew and troops had been transferred to a coaster, and she was cut adrift.

Royal Sovereign under Capt. T.J. Aldis, who received the D.S.O. for gallantry at this time, made a total of six voyages, four to Dunkirk and two to La Panne, embarking a total of 11,500 troops mostly at night. She sailed each evening from Margate pier for the French coast between 28th May and 3rd June, and also attempted a daylight crossing on 1st June but as the Dunkirk entrance was blocked by two ships and she was under heavy bombing she returned to Margate without troops. On one of her crossings she assisted *Bullfinch*, whose normal run was to North French ports, to refloat from La Panne beach heavily laden with troops. She also assisted in the evacuations from St. Malo and Cherbourg, bringing back over 2,000 men and a small number of refugees.

Royal Daffodil This almost new vessel under Capt. G. Johnson brought back over 8,500 troops from Dunkirk, arriving there seven times but being unable to embark troops on two occasions. She disembarked her exhausted troops at Dover and Margate, from where she sailed at 1730 hours on the 2nd June. She was attacked by six enemy bombers at 1950 hours on the outward trip when 17.5 miles ESE of North Goodwin L.V. and was damaged by one bomb below the waterline on the starboard side. All moveable gear was shifted to port, fuel oil was transferred to the port tank, and the hole was temporarily patched with mattresses. She proceeded at half speed to Ramsgate where she arrived at 2230 hours where repairs of a more permanent nature were carried out during the next two days.

GREENFINCH was completed in Holland in 1940 and served as EMPIRE DAFFODIL during the war. She was purchased and renamed in 1946 and sold for further service in 1966, and was deleted from the register as STAR of MEDINA in 1991. MAVIS of 1946 is seen at Yarmouth below on 10th February,1962 and was sold in 1966 to Greek owners. She is still trading today in Greece as LIMNOS.

Queen of Thanet She made two trips to Dunkirk in the early part of the evacuation, bringing home several hundred men on each occasion. She also went to the aid of the cross-Channel railway passenger ship *Prague* with over 3,000 men on board, transferring 2,000 to herself and landing them at Margate. She made one final trip to Dunkirk bringing out 100 troops and 47 wounded stretcher cases, to give a total of 4,000 men saved.

Medway Queen This famous paddler made three or four trips to Dunkirk under cover of darkness, bringing back each time her full complement of 800 troops.

The small company cargo ship *Goldfinch* under Capt. E.C. Painter then evacuated troops from St. Valery-en-Caux a few days later. She embarked 500 troops from as close in to the beach as she dared to venture and transferred them to the Stranraer passenger ship *Princess Maud*. She was soon hit twice by shells from shore batteries with splinters flying in all directions with one naval rating killed. She eventually reached Southampton, and her Master received the D.S.C. for gallantry and five others of her crew also received decorations. Subsequently *Drake, Groningen, Cormorant* and *Crane* were diverted to Western French ports including Brest to help with further evacuations; and similarly *Falcon, Woodlark* and *Stork* from Bordeaux, with *Stork* under Capt. Carey also evacuating some company staff who had moved offices several times as the fighting spread across Northern France.

The company's two largest ships, the Mediterranean traders *Philomel* and *Heron*, were requisitioned before the start of the war, with the remainder of the fleet requisitioned on or after 15th October, 1939. *Philomel* arrived at Alexandria in August,1939 and served as a transport there until January,1940 when she moved to Gibraltar and on to Freetown. Around mid-March,1940 she sailed for the Falkland Islands for a year's service as ammunition depot ship, after dry-docking at Cape Town she served in South and East Africa before sailing for Trincomalee in early 1945. Her accomodation was altered to take a native crew at Bombay before proceeding via Colombo and Trincomalee to Port Swettenham and Singapore. *Heron* was first based on Loch Kishorn and the East coast of Scotland, before sailing from Workington with an Expeditionary Force for Norway in April,1940. She was frequently under fire from aircraft and returned to Glasgow on 16th June,1940. She then sailed via Plymouth for the warmer climes of Alexandria via Cape Town and Aden. She moved to Australian waters in 1942 via Ceylon where she was attacked by three Japanese fighters with two crew injured in the attack. She was used as a stores and depot ship for the Pacific Fleet and at the end of the war after VJ-

EREGRINE of 1941 was built as EMPIRE SPINNEY on the Clyde and managed by the company uring the war. She was purchased in 1946 and is seen in Great Yarmouth Shipping Co. Ltd ›lours. She was sold in 1965 and deleted from the register in 1991. PETREL of 1945 (below) as built at Goole and was sold to Norwegian owners in 1961 and renamed as PETRELL. She as broken up in 1988.

Day she drydocked at Sydney. She then sailed for Singapore, arriving on 16th December,1945 to find her near-sister *Philomel* already in port !

Starling was heavily bombed and gunned by aircraft in October,1940 when four miles SW of San Sebastian en-route to the Mediterranean. *Cormorant* had many adventures on the East Coast in E-boat alley off Norfolk, one when taking avoiding action of torpedoed ships out of column, although her collision only resulted in a few dented plates on her regular London to Leith and Grangemouth convoys. She was also attacked by aircraft several times and had to put into the Tees and Humber when falling behind the convoy on more than one occasion. *Ortolan* was in an East coast convoy in E-boat alley in September,1940 when E-boats and bombers launched a simultaneous attack off Great Yarmouth. She was the last ship in the starboard column and had to witness the loss of four colliers to torpedoes towards the head of the convoy, and she rescued the survivors of one of these. Even in port, ships were not safe, *Falcon* overcoming fires sweeping Belfast docks, *Groningen* under Capt. C. Colin similarly at Liverpool and *Lleuwarden* at London.

Capt. Owen Morris commanded *Zamalek* (ex *Halcyon* of 1921) while serving as a Convoy Rescue Ship based at Gourock and was awarded the decoration of D.S.O. for his gallant rescue operations on the notorious Russian convoy PQ17. Her sister, *Zaafaren* (ex *Philomel* of 1921) under Capt. Watson was also based there in the same capacity, managed by General Steam during the war but still owned by Khedeval Mail Co. Ltd of Egypt. She also sailed in convoy PQ17 and was sunk by bombs from aircraft on 5th July,1942, settling by the stern in eight minutes, with her 98 crew and survivors from other ships picked up by sister *Zamalek*.

Fauvette of 1935 spent most of the war in the Mediterranean as an A.S.I.S. (Armament Supply Issuing Ship), first at Gibraltar and then at Malta under Capt. George Kelly. Four valuable company ships set out in convoy for Gibraltar in August,1941, of which only one returned safely home. *Stork* under Capt. R.J. Carey was sunk on the outward leg, while two more were lost in a single day in the returning convoy HG73 from Gibraltar on 26th September,1941. *Lapwing* had picked up some of the survivors of the MacAndrews' *Cortes* on the previous day, only to be torpedoed herself by U124 killing Capt. Hyam, twenty of her crew and three gunners. *Petrel* was sunk while sailing in the adjoining column with 22 brave men lost although Capt. Klemp survived to fight again. The sole company survivor was *Starling* under Capt. C.T. Stone, which had gallantly rescued survivors of another MacAndrews' ship *Cervantes* and *Springbank* of Bank Line which had been

ORTOLAN of 1945 was completed as EMPIRE SEABRIGHT at Goole and purchased in 1951. She was sold to Greek owners in 1958 and sank near the Alida Shoal some 180 miles East of Singapore on 14th January,1971 (A. Duncan) ALBATROSS of 1943 (below) was a wartime 'Hansa' type and was purchased by the company in 1947 for Mediterranean services. She was sold in 1958 and broken up at Hong Kong at the end of 1968 (A. Duncan)

commissioned as a Fighter Catapult Ship. Despite the latter's prescence,HG73 lost nine out of its 25 ships that had sailed out of the Rock of Gibraltar for Liverpool.

Moss-Hutchison Line, the company's Mediterranean arm, lost four stout ships to enemy action. *Kavak* was lost in the early hours of 2nd December,1940 in convoy HX90 from Halifax(NS). U101 sank her in mid-Atlantic with the loss of Capt. Napier and 24 of his crew. *Kantara,* after dispersing in mid-Atlantic from a convoy encountered the raiding battlecruisers *Scharnhorst* and *Gneisenau* on 22nd February,1941. *Gneisenau's* salvos wrecked havoc in the Master's cabin of *Kantara*, but radio messages were still sent from the radio room next door, although jammed by the battlecruiser. Capt. H. W. Weston had ordered the ship's small calibre gun to reply to the salvos. After the sinking, all of the crew were rescued by the battlecruiser and transferred to a supply ship. The Master and three other crew members were commended by the King in 1946 for bravery in the face of huge odds. *Hatasu* was torpedoed by U431 when 600 miles east of Cape Race on 2nd October,1941, the survivors drifted helplessly for two weeks in open boats through gales, high seas and low temperatures. When picked up by escorts of an eastbound convoy, only a few were left alive suffering from severe exposure, but forty of her crew had died. *Etrib* was the last Moss-Hutchison loss when torpedoed by U552 in mid-June,1942 in the 23-ship convoy HG84 of Mediterranean traders which had sailed from Gibraltar on 9th June. Enemy agents had reported the sailing and Focke-Wolf Condor aircraft had directed the U-boats to the convoy's position. Two other Mediterranean traders from Ellermans' fleets were lost and one from the MacAndrews' fleet.

Crane under Capt. G. Kelly took part in the landings in the Azores in 1943. Company ships were present at the North African landings in November,1942, and at Sicily in July,1943, with *Procris* of Moss-Hutchison under Capt. Wigg taking part in the landings in Southern France in 1944 after D-Day. *Drake* (Capt. Pirch), *Oriole* (Capt. Wighting), *Ortolan* (Capt. Davis) and *Goldfinch* (Capt. Lowe) were used as cased petrol carriers for over a month after the D-Day landings in Normandy on voyages from Southampton, Poole, Plymouth and Milford Haven to the landing beaches. *Goldfinch* continued in the same capacity supplying the Allied effort in the Low Countries through Antwerp and Rotterdam, and was, in fact, the first company ship to dock at Hamburg since 1939 when she moved up the Elbe on 25th July,1945. *Crane* under Capt. Painter became a military stores carrier from August,1944 on voyages from Southampton, Tilbury and Grimsby to Continental ports. The last two company war losses were *Auk* on 24th July,1944 to a mine in the

The excursion paddle steamer LORNA DOONE was built in 1916 as a minesweeper, and converted in 1927 to the excursion ship QUEEN of KENT for the New Medway Steam Packet Co. Ltd. She was sold in 1949 to become LORNA DOONE for Southampton owners and was withdrawn at the end of the 1951 season. CRESTED EAGLE of 1938 (below) was built at Sunderland as NEW ROYAL LADY and purchased in late 1947 for P. L. A. dock cruises. She was sold in 1957 for services to Gozo from Malta and is still in service there as IMPERIAL EAGLE today. She is seen at Greenwich.

Adriatic while on a voyage from Monopoli to Ancona with cased petrol, and even after peace returned *Lleuwarden* set off a floating mine off Dieppe and sank on 24th February,1946.

The company managed four Empire 'F' class coasters between 1944 and 1946, *Empires Fable, Facility, Fang* and *Farriday*, as well as two larger coasters built by A. & J. Inglis at their Pointhouse yard on the Clyde, *Empire Spinney* and *Empire Gat*. The former was purchased by the company in 1946 and renamed *Peregrine*, while the latter went to the G. A. Gibson & Co. Ltd fleet as *Borthwick* in 1947. The German motor coaster *Adler* built in 1938 was taken in prize in May,1945 at Vordingborg in Denmark, and then managed by the company as *Empire Coningsby* for the Ministry of War Transport until her sale to Dutch owners in 1946. The company also managed a deepsea 'Liberty' ship *Sammex*, with her London crew being replaced by a Geordie crew in 1947 when she was purchased by W. A. Souter & Co. Ltd of Newcastle, for whom she tramped the world for four years.

The above accounts can only be a snapshot of the company fleet's activity during the long years of war, but they bring home those extraordinarily dangerous times. The long list of ships that did not make it back to port follows, and the many brave men that were lost was a terrible price to pay to avoid being put under the tyranny of a German dictator, and yet who had been allowed to delude an entire nation of people. There are lessons for the future of all nations here.

WORLD WAR II LOSSES
GENERAL STEAM

8.12.1939 *Merel* Mined/sunk off Ramsgate, only 2 survivors.
12.5.1940 *Roek* Mined/sunk off Vlaardingen o.v. Rotterdam/London.
20.5.1940 *Mavis* Bombed/sunk off Calais o.v. London/Dunkirk.
28.5.1940 *Queen of the Channel* Bombed/sunk o.v. Dunkirk/Dover
31.5.1940 *Crested Eagle* Bombed at Dunkirk, beached, total loss.
24.6.1940 *Kingfisher* Torpedoed/sunk in E. Channel by E-boat o.v. MilfordHaven/London.
13.7.1940 *Mallard* Torpedoed/sunk off Cherbourg o.v. Newlyn/London.
9.12.1940 *Royal Sovereign* Mined/sunk near Barry o.v. Troon/Penarth.
22.8.1941 *Stork* Torpedoed/sunk 100 m W of Figueira de Foz o.v. Preston/Gibraltar. 19 lost.

26.9.1941	*Lapwing*	Torpedoed/sunk in position 47 48'N 23 45'W o.v. Lisbon/Glasgow.
26.9.1941	*Petrel*	Torpedoed/sunk in position 47 40'N 23 28'W o.v. Oporto/Bristol.
5.7.1942	*Zaafaren*	Bombed/sunk in convoy PQ17 o.v. Glasgow to Rejkjavik and Russia (managed by the company)
24.7.1944	*Auk*	Mined/sunk in Adriatic o.v. Monopoli / Ancona with petrol.
24.2.1946	*Lleuwarden*	Mined/sunk off Dieppe.

MOSS - HUTCHISON LINE

23.6.1940	*Kufra*	Collision/sunk 60 miles NW of Bayonne o.v. Bordeaux to Bayonne on Admiralty service.
3.9.1940	*Philotis*	Collision/sunk 8 miles NW of St. Govens L.V. o.v. Swansea to Lisbon.
2.12.1940	*Kavak*	Torpedoed/sunk in position 55 N 19 30'W o.v. Demerara & Bermuda to Newport with bauxite & pitch. 25 lost.
7.12.1940	*Lormont*	Collision/sunk off the Humber while acting as a guardship.
22.2.1941	*Kantara*	Shelled/sunk by *Gneisenau* in mid-Atlantic o.v. London &Tyne to Barbados, Trinidad & Demerara with general.
2.10.1941	*Hatasu*	Torpedoed/sunk about 600m E of Cape Race o.v. Manchester/New York in ballast. 40 lost.
15.6.1942	*Etrib*	Torpedoed/sunk in position 43 18'N 17 38'W o.v. Carthagena & Gibraltar to Liverpool, 4 lost.

POST-WAR DECLINE

The much reduced fleet gradually got back into its stride again at the end of 1945 and beginning of 1946 with the return of requisitioned ships. The fleet was bolstered during the years 1943/46 by a dozen new coasters from the yards of Henry Robb, Henry Scarr and Goole Shipbuilding & Engineering, including the purchase of *West Coaster* built in 1938 for British Isles Coasters Ltd for the grain trade of Joseph Rank Ltd. She made the first of her regular voyages up the Rhine to Cologne for the company in 1946, and in 1950 was renamed *Mallard*, the 1944 ship of that name having been transferred to the Great Yarmouth Shipping Co. Ltd as *Norwich Trader* in 1948. *Kingfisher* of 1944 from the Henry Robb yard at Leith and her sister *Stork* were the first British coasters to be built where every rating had his own cabin. *Corncrake* and *Redstart* were sisters of 730 grt from the same yard in 1946, with *Corncrake* soon in trouble from a grounding on the Norfolk coast in December, 1948 but she was towed off the next day little damaged by a Yarmouth tug.

However more ships were still needed, and two ex-German 'Hansa' types had been purchased in 1947 for the Mediterranean trades and renamed *Albatross* and *Sheldrake*, and remarkably two ex-German ships built as far back as 1912 and taken in prize at Hamburg in 1945 were purchased and renamed *Woodwren* and *Ringdove*. This latter pair of German war reparation vessels had previously plied the Rhine for their German owners and were used by the company on a London to Dunkirk service. They had funnels which collapsed inwards to negotiate the Rhine bridges, however when they were lowered they disappeared completely from view, and Deptford yard engineers had to be called in to extricate them. The previously managed *Empire Seabright* was also taken into the fleet as *Ortolan* in 1951.

WOODWREN was built in 1912 for German owners at Stettin, and was acquired in 1947 as war reparations, having been taken in prize at Hamburg. She had seen service on the Rhine and her funnel was able to be lowered. She was cut down and used as a coal hulk at Gravesend in 1953. Her identical sister RINGDOVE (below) was purchased as war reparations at the same time and was broken up at Bo'ness in 1950.

CORNCRAKE of 1946 was built by the Henry Robb yard at Leith and is seen off South Shields in February,1966 after completion of her refit at Tyne Dock Engineering Ltd. She was sold to Canadian owners in 1967 and deleted from the register in 1995. Her sister REDSTART (below) of 1946 was sold to Greek owners in 1967 and sank off Libya on 8th February,1977.

ROYAL SOVEREIGN was launched at the Denny yard on 7th May,1948 and completed in time for the 1948 summer season. She was sold in 1967 for conversion for Dover/Zeebrugge freight services as AUTOCARRIER running for Townsend Thoresen. She was sold to Italian owners in 1974 for Bay of Naples service as ISCHIA, a role she continues to play today.
ROYAL EAGLE of 1932 operated in post-war years only until the end of the 1950 season. She is seen below reversing in the Pool of London with QUEEN of the CHANNEL at Tower Hill pier. (P.A. Vicary)

The newbuilding replacement programme began with orders for eight new coasters, placed with British yards and which were completed in the years 1947/50 as *Laverock, Seamew, Woodcock, Grebe, Ptarmigan, Auk, Hirondelle* and *Swift*. The latter was launched by Mrs. J. W. Coats, wife of a director, on 15th August,1950 at the Victoria yard of Henry Robb Ltd, Leith and was completed before the end of the year, and with *Hirondelle* was completed to an engines-aft design. The first five of this programme had three holds and hatches served by derricks on two masts, with engines placed amidships - a design that was to hold sway with the final group of seven ships completed for the company between 1953 and 1957.

On the excursion trades, the almost new *Royal Sovereign* and *Queen of the Channel* and *Crested Eagle* of 1925 had sadly become war losses, and with peaceful times once more, *Royal Eagle* restarted services to Southend, Margate and Ramsgate on 8th June, 1946 and was joined by *Golden Eagle* and *Royal Daffodil* in the summer of 1947. Two new motor excursion ships to be fitted with wide sponsons and able to make French coast excursions were then ordered with a deck capacity of 2,000 passengers to be ready for the 1948 and 1949 seasons. *Royal Sovereign* delivered in 1948 was the slightly larger of the pair at 1851 grt compared to *Queen of the Channel* at 1472 grt, both from the famous Denny yard at Dumbarton. However this meant the death knell of the much loved *Golden Eagle* of 1909 at the end of the 1949 season, and *Royal Eagle* of 1932 at the end of the 1950 season. The summer excursion fleet in 1951 was down to five ships including a new *Crested Eagle*, formerly *Royal Lady*, for the shorter haul excursions, and the large new *Royal Sovereign* and *Queen of the Channel* of 1948/49, *Royal Daffodil* of 1939 and the paddler *Medway Queen* of 1924.

The summer excursion fleet wintered pre-war at the company's **Deptford Yard**, where a fresh coat of paint was applied in Spring. During the war some three hundred men were employed at the yard, not only repairing ships afloat and dry-docking the company fleet but also building the first tank landing craft on the Thames, and another larger one, and two 'flak' ships. D - Day craft conversions included 36 dumb barges into self - propelled craft, alterations to more than a dozen landing craft, and dry-docking of tugs and other small craft. The storing and manning of engineering personnel for the company's ships scattered all over the world was also done from Deptford. The biggest job undertaken by the yard after the war was the re-conversion of *Royal Eagle* back to summer excursion work, including the stripping out of many naval cabins from the saloon and complete renovation and redecoration of the vessel. However the workload gradually decreased as both the

TEAL of 1947 (above) was built at Goole and sold to Canadian owners in 1963. She is still in service today as IRON MAIDEN (A.Duncan). TERN of 1953 (below) had her engines aft and was given a grey hull with a blue line. She was sold in 1964 for further service and deleted from the register in 1991.

SEAMEW of 1947 had the more usual engines amidships design when completed at the S. P. Austin yard in Sunderland. She was sold for further trading in 1966 and sank after a collision in the Mediterranean on 3rd June,1974. Her sister LAVEROCK (below) was built at the same yard and was thrown aground in the river Douro on 15th November,1963 and refloated five days later with extensive damage. She was towed to Amsterdam for repairs in January,1964 and sold to Greek owners, later being broken up at La Spezia in 1980.

excursion fleet and the cargo fleet shrank, and the sale of the last three summer excursion ships *Royal Daffodil, Royal Sovereign* and *Queen of the Channel* in 1967 after Eagle Steamers had ceased trading in 1966 meant a much reduced workload of property repair and mechanical work for this very old yard dating back to 1825, which had always been company-owned.

Royal Daffodil went for scrap at Ghent at the end of 1967, *Royal Sovereign* was sold to Townsend Thoresen for a Dover to Zeebrugge freight service carrying a dozen passengers as *Autocarrier*, and *Queen of the Channel* was sold to Greek owners as *Oia*. The Chairman and directors of the company had each season taken a large party of guests for a day excursion usually on *Royal Daffodil*, and the staff also had their own annual summer excursion. The New Medway Steam Packet Co. Ltd ceased operations from the Medway at the end of 1963, and their last paddler *Medway Queen* of 1924, was sold for use as a clubhouse on the river Medina on the Isle of Wight.

In pre-war days, the re-export trade of goods, originally from the British Empire and other countries, from London to Europe was worth £60M annually and was an important part of British exports at around 18%. These goods included non-perishable commodities for France, Belgium, Holland and Germany. This trade continued in post-war years, but gradually decreased due to higher unloading charges at London compared to Rotterdam, Antwerp and Hamburg. The London terminii of the company routes in post-war years were at St. Katharine's Dock and London Docks on the North side, and Surrey Commercial Docks on the south side, and on any day a dozen of the company's ships could be seen loading or unloading for the Continent at these locations.

The company managed the troopship *Empire Parkeston* of 6893 grt from 1947 to 1961 for the Ministry of Defence. She had been built as the three-funnelled *Prince Henry* in 1930 by Cammell, Laird & Co. Ltd for Vancouver services but had not been successful. She and one of her two sisters, *Prince David*, moved to the East Coast for various cruise services out of Boston, New York and Miami to Bermuda, Nassau, Havana and the Caribbean. *Prince Henry* was chartered to and later owned by the Clarke Steamship Co. Ltd of Montreal but was laid-up at Halifax(NS) on the outbreak of war. She was overhauled at Southampton after purchase by the Ministry of War Transport in the summer of 1946, and sailed from Harwich for the first time in March,1947 to the Hook of Holland with troops. Her passenger complement was 813 troops in three-tiered bunks and cabin accomodation for 182 officers and families. Her paint scheme initially was black hull and twin black funnels, one of the latter having been removed during the overhaul, with

PTARMIGAN of 1948 (above) was built at Grangemouth and sold for further service in 1963. She was broken up at Rijeka in October,1982 as RABAC. Her sister WOODCOCK came from the same yard and was sold to Yugoslavian owners in 1964. She was broken up at Rijeka in June,1984 as ORJULA.

AUK was completed by the S. P. Austin yard in Sunderland in 1949 and sold to Greek owners in 1965. She was hulked in the Great Bitter Lake in Egypt in 1993 (A. Duncan). GREBE of 1948 (below) came from the Henry Robb yard at Leith and arrived at Newport for scrap on 18th October,1967.

grey superstructure, changed later to a grey hull with a blue trooping band and finally in the late 1950s her funnels were changed to troopship yellow with black tops. She served in Egypt during the Suez Canal crisis of 1956, and arrived at Harwich for the last time on 26th September,1961 flying a long paying-off pennant, and was scrapped at Spezia during 1962.

In 1950 the average size of the company's ships was around 1,000 grt, only slightly less than the average at the turn of the century but greater than the average of 400 grt of the company paddle steamers in 1850. The post-war fleet ranged in size from the 278 grt of the Rhine river trader *Alouette* to the largest member of the fleet, the Mediterranean trader *Heron* of 2374 grt. The company is particularly remembered at this point for its innovative use of railway boxes for the carriage of unitised cargoes to Continental ports. The ordinary share capital of the company in 1950 was £379,920 of which 80% was owned by P. & O., and the preference share capital was £367,580 mostly held in small parcels by a wide variety of institutions and individuals. Dividends of 10% were paid, and another subsidiary was formed in this year - **General Steam North France Lines Ltd** - being a renaming of the London & Dunkirk Shipping Co. Ltd.

The fortunes of the **Great Yarmouth Shipping Co. Ltd** and the **Grand Union Shipping Co. Ltd** were similar in post-war years in that they traded quite successfully for twenty years until the mid-1960s, when their fleets were reduced to a single motor coaster which were then sold off in 1970/71. The survivors of the Great Yarmouth subsidiary included the twin motor-driven sisters of *Lowestoft Trader* and *Boston Trader* built at Goole in 1934/36. Three more recently built motor coasters then joined the fleet during 1948/51, with the parent company transferring *Mallard* of 1944 to become *Norwich Trader* in 1948, the larger *Friargate* was purchased in 1950 from Hull Gates Shipping Co. Ltd to become *Yarmouth Trader*, and an Empire 'F' class coaster was purchased a year later to become *Lynn Trader*. Goole was a frequent loading port for services to London, Dunkirk and Boulogne. In 1956 the new Dutch-built motor coaster *Arbon* became the last member of this East Anglian fleet when she was purchased and renamed *Norfolk Trader*. In 1960 the company had a fleet of six coasters, two steam tugs and 22 barges, and *Norfolk Trader* sailed on until sold for further trading in 1970.

Two further steam coasters had joined the Grand Union subsidiary in 1940 and 1946 as *Blisworth* and *Kilworth*, built as far back as 1902 and 1911, and both were sold in 1950. Two new motor coasters joined from the Burntisland yard in 1946 as *Bosworth* and *Knebworth* of 1070 dwt and were

HIRONDELLE of 1950 was built at Leith by Henry Robb Ltd and sold to Canadian owners in 1966. In 1993 she was donated to the Royal Canadian Navy for target practice. Her sister SWIFT (below) from the same yard was sold to Yugoslavian owners in 1967 and foundered to South of Cyprus in May,1982.

LAPWING of 1944 was built at Goole. She sustained extensive damage when in collision in the Thames on 22nd March,1967, repairs were uneconomical and she arrived a week later at Grays in Essex for scrap. WOODWREN of 1954 (below) was built as EDDYSTONE for the Clyde Shipping Co. Ltd and purchased in 1956. She was sold in 1969 to Yugoslavian owners and broken up at Split in July,1988.

similar to many other coasters in the parent company, and Coast Lines, Everard and Hull Gates fleets. The first *Marsworth* was sold in 1949 and replaced at the same time by the motor coaster *Somersetbrook* of 623 dwt built in 1947 from the fleet of Comben Longstaff & Co. Ltd, but she was unfortunately sunk by collision in thick fog near Great Yarmouth on 26th November,1953. A third *Marsworth* was purchased in the following year as the motor coaster *Brier Rose* of 767 dwt built in 1952 by the Lewis yard in Aberdeen, and the final new ship for the fleet was *Blisworth* of 1375 dwt from the Hall yard in Aberdeen in 1957. *Bosworth* was nearly lost just before Christmas,1957 when she was hove-to in a severe gale with a heavy list when 150 miles to SW of Lindesnes, Norway. The Scandinavian trader *Narva* owned by Glen & Co. of Glasgow went to her aid but was tragically lost with all hands while on a voyage from Sweden to Grangemouth with woodpulp. *Bosworth* was subsequently towed into Aberdeen by a trawler, and resumed trading in the four-ship fleet. The fleet was beginning to decline by the mid-1960s and *Blisworth* was transferred to Mediterranean trading, ranging from Casablanca in Morocco to the Greek islands of the Aegean. She was the last survivor when she was sold to other British owners in April,1971. Funnel colours were yellow with a black top and 'RL' in black, and the London terminus was in Regent Canal Dock.

An unusual but regular cargo carried by the company ships for over fifty years was clean seawater from the Bay of Biscay for the London Aquarium. Around 100 tons of seawater at a time was picked up by several of the company's Bordeaux ships and brought back to the Thames. Water barges then took it along the Regents Canal for essential use by the Aquarium's marine creatures and fish. The last ship to carry this regular cargo was *Adjutant*, completed on the Wear in 1954 by S. P. Austin & Son Ltd during her twelve year career with the company. She was one of seven similar ships built for the company during 1953/57, the others being *Whitewing, Ringdove, Woodlark, Gannet, Heron* and *Sandpiper*. *Tern* completed in 1953 had engines aft and was fitted exclusively for the carriage of chilled and frozen meat. She was given a grey hull to minimise heating of the holds during warm weather. This was also the year of the death of Robert Kelso, who had retired as Chairman in 1949 and been succeeded by J. W. Coats, who had joined the company as a freight clerk in 1907 and had been made a director in 1937. When J. W. Coats retired, two joint Chairmen and Managing Directors were appointed in Mr. Hooper, son of Capt. H. B. Hooper (Vice-Chairman 1902 - 1923) and in Reginald G. Grout, secretary since 1941 and a director since 1946. On the tragic death of Mr. Hooper, Reginald G. Grout remained as sole Chairman of the company.

WHITEWING of 1953 saw service for the company in South and West African ports. She was sold to Yugoslavian owners in 1964 and broken up at Rijeka in June,1983 as ORUDA (A.Duncan). Her sister RINGDOVE of 1954 (below), also from the Ailsa yard, was sold in 1967 and broken up at Split in December,1983 as OTOK.

ADJUTANT was launched at the S. P. Austin yard in Sunderland on 5th January,1954 and fitted with a Sulzer diesel engine built at the Winterthur works in Switzerland. She was sold to Yugoslavian owners in 1966 and renamed GALIOLA and broken up at Split in January,1983. GANNET of 1956 (below) was built at Grangemouth and sold to Canadian owners in 1968 and renamed SARAH. She struck a wreck and sank in Anguilla Bay during a hurricane on 7th November,1984.

SARAH (ex GANNET of 1956) at St. John's (NF) with Signal Hill and Cabot Tower in the distance.

Heron under Capt. Painter and *Woodlark* under Capt. Gordon Renshawe were often on the Bordeaux wine trade from London, while the others were switched around the Hamburg, Rotterdam, Antwerp and north French Channel ports services. A further coaster was purchased from the rapidly decreasing fleet of the Clyde Shipping Co. Ltd in 1956 and renamed *Woodwren* - this was *Eddystone* of 1180 dwt built by the Grangemouth Dockyard two years previously - and which had a 13-year career with the company on the Bordeaux run before being sold to Yugoslav owners in 1969. *Whitewing* spent well over a year trading in South African waters in 1958/59, on a service from Mozambique and South Africa to Angola, Belgian Congo, Nigeria, Ghana and particularly to Takoradi on the Ashanti Gold Coast. Similarly, Coast Lines had a much lengthier involvement in the South and West African coastal trades between 1949 and 1966. P. & O., who owned both of these companies by 1971, formed a joint company with South African-based Union Acceptances Ltd to provide new investment for South African companies in the fields of mining, shipping, transport and merchant banking.

The Mediterranean trades were concentrated on the **Moss - Hutchison Line** in post-war years, with seven new ships delivered from British yards during 1947/52 of between 3200 and 3600 grt as *Memphis*, *Kantara*, *Karnak*, *Amarna*, *Assiout*, *Kypros* and *Tabor*. The much smaller General Steam coasters *Hirondelle* and *Swift* were transferred in 1948 to Moss - Hutchison to become *Landes* and *Lormont* respectively, and the last General Steam Mediterranean trader *Heron* was also transferred in 1956 to become *Kufra*, and was sold in 1959. The seven new Moss-Hutchison ships traded to the Mediterranean throughout the 1960s decade, with *Memphis*, *Kantara* and *Karnak* sold in 1971/72 and the remaining quartet by 1976. P. & O. decided to register two new Aberdeen-built Mediterranean traders under Moss-Hutchison in 1971 as *Melita* and *Makaria*. The former ship was launched in June,1971 and completed in November of that year, with *Makaria* launched by Mrs. Hawkes, wife of a director of the company, on 16th November,1971 and completed in February,1972; and they traded until their sale to Mexican owners in 1979.

The General Steam fleet of North European traders was still of reasonable size at the beginning of 1960 at 38 steam and motor-driven ships, which included the management of the Harwich - Hook of Holland twin-funnelled troopship *Empire Parkeston*, built in 1930 as the three-funnelled *Prince Henry* by Cammell,Laird & Co. Ltd with two sets of Parsons geared steam turbines. There were only two other steamers in the fleet, *Philomel* which had been built as *Groningen* in 1928 and renamed in 1958, and *Starling*

SANDPIPER of 1957 was built at Leith by the Henry Robb yard and sold to Canadian owners ten years later. She was broken up at Gadani Beach in April,1989 (J. Clarkson). WOODLARK of 1956 (Below) was built at Grangemouth and sold in 1969 and was laid-up at Marchwood near Southampton in the early 1970s. She arrived at Sittingbourne for scrap in May,1979.

HERON of 1957 was built by the Chas. Hill yard at Bristol and sold for further service in 1969. She disappeared on a voyage from Piraeus to Livorno in December,1973 (Real Photos). SWALLOW of 1947 (below) was taken over at Amsterdam as TEXELSTROOM on 24th February,1961 having been built at Aalborg as DORRIT CLAUSEN. She was sold in 1967 and sank off Navarino Bay on 13th January,1968.

of 1930. The latter arrived at a Grays scrapyard in August,1960, and *Philomel* followed in May,1961. Typical of the many sales of company vessels for further trading at this time was *Fauvette* of 1935, sold in 1963 and renamed *Southern Star*, and resold in 1969 to supply Grand Cayman Island in the Caribbean as *Island Supplier*, which she continued to do until around 1990.

The company had moved from Trinity Square into purpose-built new headquarters in 1960 at Three Quays, Tower Hill on the site of the earlier Brewers Quay owned by the company. The company entered the container age when it began operating its **Hinterland Container Service** in 1958 from Felixstowe, using 10 feet long containers to import scientific and optical goods from Germany. By 1965, the company had joint containerised services to Holland and Germany in conjunction with Associated Humber Lines, William H. Muller N.V. of Holland and Argo Reederei of Germany. In 1968 the company formed a subsidiary, **European Unit Routes,** specifically to handle the short-sea container trades with a three times weekly service between Tilbury and Dunkirk in each direction. However the decline in the fleet during the 1960s was just as dramatic as that in Coast Lines, and for the same reason - the massive growth of road haulage. However the fleet was bolstered when a second-hand Dutch owned coaster was taken over at Amsterdam on 24th February,1961 and renamed *Swallow*. She was of 1463 grt and had been built at Aalborg in 1947 as *Dorrit Clausen*. By 1965 the last of a group of six new motor coasters *Oriole, Ortolan, Albatross, Avocet, Petrel* and *Plover* had joined the fleet, which then numbered under thirty vessels. This last sextet had fully-automated cargo handling systems and the latest navigational aids, and were known by their crews as 'push-button' ships. They served on the routes to Hamburg, Rhine ports and North French ports. The company was running a twice weekly cargo service from Southampton to Le Havre using *Oriole* following the closure of the Southern Railway Company passenger/cargo service in May,1964. However this was immediately threatened by a three-ship operation by newcomer Townsend Thoresen.

General Steam backed by P. & O. decided to compete on both the passenger and cargo sides of the Southampton to Le Havre service. Staff were seconded from London to Southampton ready for the introduction of two new vessels for a new **Normandy Ferries** venture, formed jointly with French-based S.A.G.A. (Soc. Anonyme de Gerance et d'Armement). British-flagged *Dragon* under Southern Ferries and French-flagged *Leopard* owned by S.A.G.A. went into service in 1967/68 after completion at Nantes with accomodation for 850 passengers and 250 cars (or a mixture of lorries and cars). Credit for much of the preparatory work for the new venture at

SHELDRAKE was built as MANCHESTER VANGUARD for Manchester Liners Ltd Great Lakes service in 1956. She was the first vessel into the St. Lawrence Seaway in 1959. She was purchased by the company in 1963 and sold five years later, eventually being broken up at Hong Kong in May,1985. She is seen at Newcastle in May,1963 (above). Her sister PHILOMEL was built as MANCHESTER VENTURE and purchased in 1961. She was sold in 1968 and renamed BAT TIRAM and was beached after explosion and fire in her cargo in August,1972 while on a voyage from Rijeka to Haifa and broken up at Piraeus in September,1972.

ORTOLAN of 1964 was built by J. Lewis at Aberdeen and is seen at Newcastle on 17th November, 1972 (above) and with a GSNC houseflag on her foremast below. She was sold to British owners in 1979 and renamed MARAL R. She left Berwick on 26th August,1987 and after a galley fire drifted down the Northumberland coast on fire to ground on Seaton Sluice beach. She was broken up as she lay during that winter. (J. Clarkson)

ORIOLE at Krefel on the Rhine ready to unload NAAFI stores for the British Army with warehouse supervisor Mr. R. Seed overseeing operations. (G.S.N.C. Newsletter)

ORIOLE of 1963 was built by the J. Lewis yard at Aberdeen and sold for further service in 1977, and sank off Collo in Algeria on 4th March,1983 after a collision had cracked her hull. (A. Duncan). PETREL of 1965 (below) was built by the J. Bolson yard at Poole and sold in 1978. She is still in service as the Panamanian flag LATONA.

Southampton went to William J. Wilson OBE who joined the company in 1930. He worked first in London and Antwerp before going to the Moss Hutchison Agency in Alexandria in the late 1940s, becoming Manager of the Bordeaux office from 1953 to 1965 before secondment to Southampton. An Irish service from Le Havre to Rosslare followed, plus an order for a much larger ferry of 11,000 grt for a Southampton - Lisbon - Casablanca service. The latter was delivered from the same Nantes shipyard under the name of *Eagle* in 1971, and was joined by the freight ro-ro ferry *Falcon* on a year-round service to Portugal from Southampton in the same year. Readers will notice that all four of these new ferries used traditional General Steam names, a connection that was later strengthened by P. & O. with their ferries *Panther, Tiger* and *Lion* under their own name of P. & O. Ferries Ltd from 1976.

An interesting new ship and new trade came under the management of the company in 1967 when *Tanmerack* of 2480 dwt was delivered to the Charter Shipping Co. Ltd, a P. & O. subsidiary, and sailed with a 'Navvies' crew. She had three large derricks suitable for the handling of timber, and was on charter to Canadian Pacific for timber cargoes from Quebec to Liverpool. She continued on this trade until sold in 1973 to Coe Metcalf Ltd and was renamed *Quickthorn*. *Albatross* delivered 6,500 gallons of seawater at Shoreham in August,1971 for onward delivery by road tanker to Pinewood Studios in connection with the making of a film. She was on her regular wine run from Bordeaux to London and picked up the seawater from the Bay of Biscay, from where regular supplies used to be picked up for delivery to London Aquarium. Road haulage firm Thomas Allen Ltd within the Coast Lines Group provided the road tankers. General Steam also had for many years a road haulage subsidiary of its own, **Blackmore's Motor Transport Co. Ltd,** and other non-shipowning subsidiaries included **Thos. Trapp & Sons Ltd** (freight forwarders and agents for the onward delivery of imported wine), **A.U.L. Ascania Unit Loaders Ltd**, and **Three Quays Marine Services Ltd**. *Oriole* had moved from the Southampton/Le Havre weekly cargo run to the London/Rhine ports service in 1968. This had calls at Rochester, Felixstowe, Duisburg, Krefeld and Cologne, with a Rhine pilot always carried between Dordrecht and Cologne as the river had notoriously bad currents and bridges. A particularly bad stretch was at Duisburg, and when the river was low groundings had to be avoided, with the opposite problem of having to lower her radio and radar masts to negotiate bridges at speed when the river was in spate. The Rhine ports service ceased in 1971 when it was taken over by A. Kirsten of Hamburg, who had been operating a Rhine Trade Pool Agreement with the company for the previous ten years.

PLOVER of 1965 was built by the J. Bolson yard at Poole and sold to the Ramsey Steamship Co Ltd of the Isle of Man in 1971 and renamed BEN VEEN. On 18th October,1988 as the British MEDINA D she capsized and sank off the Suffolk coast while on a voyage from Rouen to Great Yarmouth (J. Clarkson) ALBATROSS of 1965 (below) was built by J. Lewis at Aberdeen and sold in 1976 and is still in service today as the Panamanian-flag DISTA.

AVOCET of 1965 was built by J. Lewis at Aberdeen and sold in 1976 to Cypriot owners. As HAMADA she struck a submerged object off Ras Banas, Egypt on 28th June,1993 and sank the next day on a voyage from Jeddah to Suez.
DRAGON was built in 1967 by the Dubigeon yard at Nantes for Southern Ferries Southampton to Le Havre service, managed by General Steam staff at Southampton and with a 'Navvies' crew. She was absorbed into the P. & O. Ferries fleets as IONIC FERRY in 1986, and sold for trading in Greek waters as VISCOUNTESS M in 1992. She was renamed CHARM M in 1995 and runs today in Black Sea waters as MEMED ABASHIDZE.

A large clear-out of the 'Navvies' fleet had occurred with only ten coasters left by the end of 1968. By February,1971 when Coast Lines was sold for £5.6M to P. & O., General Steam was about to become 100% owned by the deep-sea company when the remainder of the ordinary and preference shares were acquired. The company had only six coasters left with *Plover* of 1965 in course of sale to the Ramsey Steamship Co. Ltd, Ramsey, Isle of Man to become *Ben Veen*. P. & O. renamed the company **General Steam Navigation (Trading) Ltd,** and the five-ship fleet continued to carry unit-load, containers and general cargo including the important brandy and wine imports from Bordeaux until they were all sold during 1976/79. The last to be sold of this quintet later suffered a serious galley fire while off Berwick on the Northumberland coast on 26th August,1987 while named *Maral R*, and drifted down the coast until being grounded on Seaton Sluice beach. The former *Ortolan* was broken up during that winter as she lay.

Douglas Louis James Mortelman OBE had suceeded Reginald G. Grout as Chairman of the company in 1964 and was its last Chairman in 1973, recently he has died peacefully in September,1998 aged 89 years. He joined as a clerk in 1928, becoming a director in June,1951 and was a worthy successor to a long line of Chairmen including Hylton Jolliffe, Richard White, W.J. McAlister, Lord Inchcape, Robert Kelso, J.W. Coats, R.G. Grout and many others. John R. Turner, previously Managing Director of Coast Lines, was appointed Managing Director and Deputy Chairman in 1971 of the company. His assistant at Coast Lines, Norman Burrell, was appointed to the General Steam Board as Deputy Managing Director, and the Coast Lines Marine Superintendent Capt. Ronald Morrison was also moved into the P.& O. Short Sea Shipping set-up. Capt. Howgego, Marine Superintendent of General Steam, retired in September,1971. He had joined the company in 1940 and became Assistant Marine Superintendent to Capt. Odell in 1952. He became Marine Superintendent in 1959 on the death of his chief, and was also Marine Manager for the new passenger ferries until this was transferred to Southampton in 1970 under Capt. Frank Smith. Capt. Howgego's father had also served in General Steam vessels at the turn of the century before he became a Trinity House pilot.

There are still several former General Steam coasters in existence as we approach a new Millennium. The oldest by far at 125 years is the former *Honfleur* built in 1874 for the London & South Western Railway Company, and which was briefly owned by General Steam as *Fauvette* in 1924 before being sold to trade under the Turkish flag for the last 75 years. Others include the former *Stork* completed in April,1945 by Henry Robb Ltd and now the

The final EAGLE of 1971 ran on a Southampton to Lisbon, Cadiz and Tangiers passenger service. (G.S.N.C. Newsletter)

Greek *Nikos Litochoron*, *Mavis* of 1946 as the Greek *Limnos*, *Teal* of 1947 as the formidably named *Iron Maiden*, *Crested Eagle* built in 1938 as *New Royal Lady* is still in service at Malta as *Imperial Eagle*, the much-loved excursion steamer *Royal Sovereign* of 1948 is the Italian ro-ro ferry *Ischia* in the Bay of Naples, as well as the more recent *Albatross* and *Petrel* of 1965 and *Tanmerack* of 1967.

The streamlined passenger ferry *Dragon* of 1967 is still running in Black Sea waters as *Memed Abashidze* managed by Denholm Ship Management, having been in Greek waters between 1992 and 1997. She is now operated by the Georgian Steamship Co. Ltd and runs between Istanbul and Black Sea ports, and has recently dry-docked at Odessa. Her larger stablemate *Eagle* now sails the beautiful waters of the Mediterranean and Caribbean as the cruiseship *The Azur*. These remarkable survivors of the long-lasting 'Navvies' fleet, which had its beginnings at the start of the 19th century, are still in service as we approach the start of the 21st century. The fleet can thus justifiably claim a long history of service spanning almost two centuries of sea trading.

The fleet lists cover the main General Steam Navigation Company fleet, as well as :-

Moss - Hutchison Line (MH)
New Medway Steam Packet Co. Ltd (NM)
Great Yarmouth Shipping Co. Ltd (GY)
Grand Union Shipping Co. Ltd (GU)
and contain the following abbreviations :-
GRT - Gross Registered Tonnage
WP - Wooden Paddlers
CP - Composite (wood/iron) Paddlers
IP - Iron Paddlers
IS - Iron Screw - Propelled Ships

APPENDIX
RECOLLECTIONS OF GOLDEN EAGLE DURING HER FINAL SEASON OF 1949

by Capt. Gordon Renshawe

I joined *Golden Eagle* (affectionately known as *'Goldie'* by her crew) in April,1949 as Second Mate at Westminster Pier for storing. She had reached forty years of age, having been built in 1909 by the famous yard of John Brown & Co. Ltd at Clydebank. Usually she lay overnight at East Lane Tier, east of Tower Bridge then moved into the Pool to sail with passengers at 0930 hours, returning from her excursions at 2130 hours. She had a huge brass wheel abaft of the funnel which made steering fairly difficult. The Thames was so polluted at this time that an hour after sailing my eyes would be smarting, and my gold cap badge and buttons would be green by Southend, and I had to take gulps of water for my throat all of the way downriver. Prior to leaving the buoys I had to supervise the crew at 0500 hours and make ready, oil and blacklead the rod and chain steering gear from bridge to aft, most of which ran under passenger seats on each side. I also had to write up the rough log for the day's journey so that the deckboy could fill in the times as we passed the points of reference, then write up the fair copy of the previous day's log. We called at Gravesend Pier, Southend at 1215 hours and Clacton at 1445 hours. If the tide was suitable we arrived at Clacton 45 minutes earlier by going over the Wallet Spit with myself standing on the paddle sponson sounding with the lead to ensure we had a fathom under us on a rising tide. We could then fit in a hour-long mid-afternoon hour trip from Clacton to Gunfleet Spit and back, which was usually packed to capacity with holidaymakers from the Essex resort.

I also had to organise the security of both gangway moorings by rushing down from the bridge on arrival at the piers. I also took the wheel from Tower Pier to Gravesend, on and off at Southend Pier and at Clacton with the Bosun at the wheel between Southend and Clacton and myself on sea watch. The Chief Officer did virtually nothing until mid-season when I complained to the Marine Superintendent and he was given the fair copy log to write up. I also had to make out the wage bill for the sixty crew and then pay it out to them on Thursdays on the return passage after Southend. My day off was Friday and I always called in at Adelaide House to get the latest Notices to Mariners. One of the jobs of the Second Mate was to take the charts (A mere formality) and clock up to the bridge before sailing. Capt. Kitto was a superb ship handler and a kindly man and entertained the passengers from the bridge wing; he also helped me to learn the Thames for future pilotage examinations.

'Goldie' had a huge wide foredeck, with a wondeful view down from the bridge, watching the Cockney passengers dancing and doing 'knees-ups', their families had been coming on excursions for generations. On arrival back in the evenings we would swing in the Tower Pool to arrive under Tower Bridge stern first. *'Goldie'* had two massive saloons and served excellent food to her passengers with the crew receiving less tasty morsels. Our accomodation was under the foredeck, and while under way we could not get to our cabins as the most popular bar, which was always full, was up forward, and we ate under the stairway usually in full view of the passengers. Of course, no visit to Southend was complete for the passengers without buying sticks of rock, whelks and 'kiss-me-quick' hats. Those that passed the day there all arrived back for the return voyage with soggy bags of chips, shrimps and whelks etc, which usually ended up on the deck for us to clear up. They were a great crowd, it was perhaps their only holiday outing of the year with entire generations of families present. All of their left-over refuse had to be swept up and bagged before we could go ashore from the buoys

Celebrities there were aplenty, including Brian Johnson, Dorothy Squires, Gilbert Harding, radio stars from 'It's that man again' programme, and the formerly glamorous musical film star of the 1920s and 1930s, Lottie Collins. Our retired radio officer, Freddie Fox, would play records or relay 'Housewives Choice' or 'Workers Playtime' from the radio, but mostly our passengers made their own music. Brian Johnson got caught out on one trip by the small imaginary black dog called 'Sooty' which was allegedly brought on board by a barman and fed dinners and biscuits under the seats, but which strangely nobody ever saw. When it was supposed to have escaped, Brian told his radio listeners of his 'Down your Way' programme to take the next excursion on *'Goldie'* to find it - great fun !

'Goldie' used to take a terrific list when something of interest was pointed out on one side of the river. On leaving Southend one evening a girl went into labour and gave birth before Greenwich. Capt Kitto broke all speed limits that night, and on the following Friday he had to register the birth at the Mercantile Marine Office at Dock Street, where he was asked if he had inspected the woman's marriage certificate - his reply was unrepeatable ! Another memorable woman passenger, a wealthy widow, had been advised by her doctor to go on a long cruise and instead took our excursion every day for the season. She would go ashore at each pier and come back loaded with sweets and fruit for the crew, with Capt. Kitto complaining one time that he had been left out, so at the next pier she bought him a huge pink whistle which he blew with great ceremony from the wing of the bridge !

Our Second Engineer was in his late 'fifties and was a very handsome man, with all of the ladies gazing down at him from the engine room top, he used to rather show off for them in his smart uniform. The engine room was a great attraction, with all of the pistons and paddle wheels visible through glass panels. When we tied up at night, the Fourth Engineer could not go ashore until he had inspected every nut in the paddle boxes. We often had to stop on passage and pull baulks of timber out of the paddle boxes. On arrival at the piers, the shore party used to run up and down with cork fenders trying to guess where Capt. Kitto would berth each day, and shouting to avoid damage.

Sir William Currie, Deputy Chairman of the great P. & O. from 1933 and long-time Chairman until he retired in 1960, came aboard one day with our General Steam Chairman, Robert Kelso. They were sunning themselves on deckchairs when our deckhand, a retired policeman, came up and asked for the sixpence deckchair charge. They both protested and told him who they were, but it made no difference - our former copper replying 'I'm the Chairman and if you don't pay a shilling you can get out of those seats' with both men then digging in their pockets and paying, very amused. We had two more former policemen aboard as barmen. Once, when approaching Margate Pier, our rotund Bosun was too energetic in throwing a heaving line ashore, overbalanced, and fell into the sea. When we got alongside, he came up the gangway dripping wet, and we bribed a little girl to go up to him to ask him to do it again ! The mid-afternoon hour trip from Margate was around the North Goodwin L.V., with the company advertising 'a possible view of France'. This was almost impossible every day, but once we saw a faint line on the horizon, and Capt. Kitto got so excited he nearly gave the game away.

All of the deckhands enjoyed their summer season, which lasted well into September, when they were paid off, and the rest of the officers and crew served on the company's cargo ships during the winter. The excursion vessels were destored either at East Lane Pier near Tower Bridge or at Deptford yard, but laid-up for the winter at the Acorn yard, Rochester of Medway Shipping. However this proved to be *'Goldie's'* last season, and we put her ashore at Whitewall Creek on the Medway, where she lay until taken to Grays in Essex for scrapping during 1951.

Thus ended the career of the best-remembered of the Thames excursion steamers in a career of 42 years which included valuable service to her country in two World Wars including the evacuation of troops from Dunkirk.

AUTHOR'S FOOTNOTE

Gordon Renshawe also served as Second Mate of the *Royal Sovereign* during the 1952 and 1953 summer excursion seasons. He then served on a dozen of the company's post-war cargo ships, being promoted to Master of the *Whitewing* in 1958. He well remembers arriving one day in the early 1950s at Southampton with 500 tons of brandy from Tonnay Charente in a coaster which the pilot thumped into the Town Pier, causing a dent in her hull. The pilot atoned for his action by buying the Master a pint at Southampton Master Mariners Club! He subsequently commanded the *Norfolk Trader, Hirondelle, Woodwren, Oriole (*on a weekly Southampton to Le Havre run with two days and nights in the French port), *Ortolan, Blisworth, Avocet, Albatross, Woodlark,* and *Heron* until June,1967 when he was given command of the new passenger ferry *Dragon* for the Southampton to Le Havre run. He also served as Master of the new cargo ship *Tanmerack* for one voyage of her regular timber run from Quebec to Liverpool in December,1968 on charter to Canadian Pacific. He later was the first Master of the much larger passenger ferry *Eagle* in March,1971 on the Southampton to Lisbon, Cadiz and Tangier run, commanding her until she was sold to Paquet Line in November,1975. He was also Master of the other P. & O. Group companies ferries *Norwave, Panther* and *Lion* until his retirement as Senior Master (Ferries) in January,1980. He lives happily today in New Milton in Hampshire.

Captain Gordon Renshawe

Company eagle motif

GENERAL STEAM NAVIGATION CO. LTD.

Name	Date Acquired * or Built	Grt	Builder	Type	Career
1. EAGLE	1824*	56	Brockelbank	WP	Built 1820 for Thames excursions
2. BELFAST	1824*	146	Belfast	WP	Built 1821 London/Rotterdam
3. ECLIPSE	1824*	88	Brent, Rotherhithe	WP	Built 1820 for Thames excursions
4. VENUS	1824*	185	Brent, Rotherhithe	WP	Built 1821 for Thames excursions 22.4.1831 Damaged in collision. Hulked in 1845.
5. BROCKELBANK	1824	126	London	WP	Built 1814 for Thames excursions
6. EARL of LIVERPOOL	1824*	168	London	WP	Built 1822 London/Ostend
7. LORD MELVILLE	1824*	171	Chester	WP	Built 1822 London/Calais
8. ROYAL SOVEREIGN	1824*	202	Brockelbank	WP	Built 1822 for Thames excursions
9. SOHO	1824*	433	London	WP	Built 1820 London/Leith
10. CITY OF LONDON	1824	213	Brockelbank	WP	Thames excursions
11. HYLTON JOLLIFFE	1824*	174		WP	London/Hamburg
12. HERO	1824*	233	Brockelbank	WP	Built 1821 for Thames excursions
13. VICTORY	1824*	160	Evans, Rotherhithe	WP	Thames excursions
14. CAMILLA	1825*	173		WP	Sold by 1847
15. ATTWOOD	1825	310	Blackwall	WP	Thames excursions
16. PRINCE FREDERICK	1825*	256		WP	Sold by 1847
17. SUPERB	1825*	125		WP	London/Ostend
18. TALBOT	1825*	100		WP	Brighton/Dieppe
19. DUKE of YORK	1826*	327	Blackwall	WP	London/Lisbon Sold to H.M. Govt. in 1830 ren. MESSENGER for Malta/Corfu mail service.
20. MAGNET	1826*	166	Limehouse	WP	Built 1825 for Thames excursions Broken up in 1847.
21. COLUMBINE	1826	393	Brockelbank	WP	Thames excursions 1855 Stranded near Rotterdam
22. GEORGE IV	1826*	341	Blackwall	WP	London/Lisbon Sold to H.M. Govt. in 1830 ren. HERMES for Malta/Corfu mail service.
23. HARLEQUIN	1826	315	Brockelbank	WP	Thames excursions Broken up 1856
24. NOTTINGHAM	1826*	101		WP	Sold by 1847
25. SIR EDWARD BANKS	1826	322	London	WP	London/Rotterdam
26. WATERLOO	1826*	233		WP	Sold by 1847
27. RAMONA	1828	356	Evans, Rotherhithe	WP	Thames excursions & other runs
28. LONDON MERCHANT	1831	330	London	WP	London/Leith
29. MONARCH	1833	516	London	WP	London/Leith Sold in 1846
30. CITY of HAMBURG	1834	518	London	WP	London/Hamburg
31. FAME	1834*	294		WP	Shoreham/Dieppe B/U c1865
32. JOHN BULL	1835	591	London	WP	London/Hamburg 1879 Converted to a coal hulk
33. BRITANNIA	1835	321	London	WP	London/Rotterdam & other runs Sold Havre SS Cie ren. SPHINX Broken up in 1847
34. RAPID	1835*	333	Greenock	WP	Built 1820 Newhaven/Dieppe Chartered from 1825
35. JUPITER	1835*	451	London	WP	Sold by 1847

	Name	Date Acquired * or Built	Grt	Builder	Type	Career
36.	MOUNTAINEER	1824*	122	London	WP	London/Ostend Chartered from 1824 Wrecked 1837 entering Shoreham
37.	CITY of EDINBURGH	1836*	301	Wigram & Green	WP	London/Leith Built 1821
38.	JAMES WATT	1836*	462	Port Glasgow	WP	Built 1822 London/Leith Broken up in 1848
39.	TOURIST	1836*	236	Perth	WP	Built 1821 London/Leith
40.	CALEDONIA	1836	706	Blackwall	WP	London/Hamburg 1864 Stranded in fog at Flamborough Head.
41.	WILLIAM JOLLIFFE	1836*	311	London	WP	Built 1826 London/Antwerp
42.	ALBION	1836*	260	Evans, Rotherhithe	WP	Built 1821 for Thames excursions
43.	DART	1836*	247	Evans, Rotherhithe	WP	Built 1823 for Thames excursions
44.	MENAI	1836*	263		WP	Shoreham/Havre
45.	GIRAFFE	1836	410	London	WP	London/Rotterdam
46.	OCEAN	1836	464	London	WP	London/Hamburg
47.	CLARENCE	1836	760	London	WP	London/Edinburgh
48.	COUNTESS of LONSDALE	1836	677	London	WP	London/Rotterdam Sold c1869.
49.	NEPTUNE	1837	599	Wigram & Green	WP	London/Hamburg Sold 1846.
50.	LEITH	1837	907	Menzies, Leith	WP	London/Leith
51.	RAINBOW	1838	407	London	IP	London/Antwerp
52.	SIR WILLIAM WALLACE	1839	190		WP	Sold by 1847
53.	WATERWITCH	1841*	481	London	WP	Built 1835 London/Hull for Humber SS Co. B/U 1855.
54.	VIVID	1841*	428	London	WP	Built 1835 London/Hull for Humber SS Co. B/U 1855.
55.	MERCURY	1841*	252		WP	Built 1834 for Star S.P. Co
56.	WILBERFORCE	1841*	610	London	WP	Built 1837 London/Hull for Humber SS Co. B/U 1856.
57.	PRINCESS ROYAL	1841	748	Wigram & Green	WP	London/Hamburg
58.	TRIDENT	1841	971	Wigram & Green	WP	London/Leith 1884 - Converted to a coal hulk.
59.	VENEZUELA	1843*	308	Greenock	WP	Built 1840 London/Havre
60.	LITTLE WESTERN	1844	431	London	CP	London to Ramsgate. Later a coal hulk at Gravesend. Collision/sunk in 1876.
61.	MAGICIAN	1844*	175	London	IP	Built 1842 Dover/Calais
62.	TRITON	1845	357	London	IP	London/Ostend 1878 - B/U.
63.	STAR	1846*	231	Limehouse	WP	Built 1834 for Star S.P. Co.
64.	LION	1847*	667	Glasgow	IP	Sold in 1883 for breaking up.
65.	ALBION(2)	1848	362	West Ham	IP	Sold in 1888 for breaking up.
66.	PRINCE of WALES	1849*	246	Miller & Ravenhill	IP	Built 1843 Sold 1880 for B/U
67.	SEINE	1849	391	C.J. Mare	IP	London/Havre 1890 Broken up.
68.	RHINE	1849	547	C.J. Mare	IP	London/Ostend 1889 Broken up.
69.	ROYAL WILLIAM	1849*	325		IP	Sold by 1875
70.	TIGER	1850*	604		WP	Built 1838 Hulked on Thames lower reach.
71.	MONARCH(2)	1850*	872		IP	Sold by 1875
72.	CONCORDIA	1851	467	Glasgow	IP	Broken up in 1887.

Name	Date Acquired * or Built	Grt	Builder	Type	Career
3. PANTHER	1851	425	C.J. Mare	IP	London/Ostend and Boulogne Broken up in 1885.
4. RAVENSBOURNE	1852*	606		IP	Sold by 1875
5. MOSELLE	1852	574	C.J. Mare	IP	Broken up in 1888.
6. EDINBURGH	1853*	741		WP	Purchased from Germanic Confederation
7. DENMARK	1853*	501		WP	Purchased from Germanic Confederation
8. HOLLAND	1853*	241	Bristol	WP	Purchased from Germanic Confederation
9. HANOVER	1853*	519		WP	Purchased from Germanic Confederation
0. NEWCASTLE	1853*	447		IP	Purchased from Germanic Confederation
1. BELGIUM	1853*	457	Bristol	WP	Purchased from Germanic Confederation
2. DRAGON	1854	535	Palmer	IS	London/Newcastle
3. RUBY	1854*	243	Blackwall	WP	Purchased from Diamond S.P. Co.
4. SAPPHIRE	1854*	238	Blackwall	IP	Purchased from Diamond S.P. Co
5. TOPAZ	1854*	141	Blackwall	WP	Purchased from Diamond S.P. Co.
6. PILOT	1854	522	London	IS	London/Boulogne 1885 Broken up
7. PIONEER	1854	413	Newcastle	IS	London/Newcastle 1877 Broken up.
8. DIAMOND	1855*	137	Blackwall	WP	Purchased from Diamond S.P.
9. DOLPHIN	1855	626	London	IP	1885 Collision/sunk.
0. EAGLE(2)	1856*	325	Northfleet	IP	Built 1853 London/Ramsgate Broken up in 1888.
1. LEO	1856*	569	Liverpool	IP	Broken up in 1880.
2. GERMANIA	1856	630	London	IS	London/Hamburg Broken up 1878
3. BRUISER	1857*	506		IS	Sold by 1875
4. WANSBECK	1857	597	Newcastle	IS	London/Newcastle 1888 Broken up
5. COLOGNE	1858	510	London	IP	London/Holland 1890 Broken up.
6. COSMOPOLITAN	1859*	526	Glasgow	IS	Stranded in 1881.
7. METROPOLITAN	1859*	521	Glasgow	IS	Broken up in 1882.
8. BOREAS	1860*	412	Stockton	IS	Dismantled in 1885.
9. SAXONIA	1860*	358	Hull	IS	Built 1855. Sold 1877 to Russia ren. NISHNI NOVGOROD
00.HARBURG	1860*				
01.LEOPARD	1860*	374	Stockton	IS	Built 1855 Hulked in 1885.
02.BERLIN	1861*	740		IP	Broken up by 1875.
03.ERA	1861	566	Palmer	IS	Broken up in 1890.
04.ELBA	1861*	620	Newcastle	IS	Built 1855 Missing in 1876
05.PERTH	1861*	595	Pt.Glasgow	WP	Built 1834 for Dundee.Perth & London SS Co. 8.11.1864 - Destroyed by fire.
06.ARNO	1861*	621	J. Reid. Pt. Glasgow	IS	Built 1851 for Liverpool & Med. SS. Co. Ltd 1854 Used as Crimean war trans-port & store ship at Eupatoria. 1866 - Wrecked.
07. NORA	1861	432	Cork	IS	Lost in 1880.
08.CHEVY CHASE	1862*	810	Napier.Glasgow	IP	Broken up in 1870.
09.SIR WALTER RALEIGH	1862*	239	Renfrew	IP	Built 1858 Purchased forThames excursions Broken up in 1891.
10.VIGILANT	1862*	257	Hull	IS	Built 1857 Broken up in 1877.

Name	Date Acquired * or Built	Grt	Builder	Type	Career
111.WATERLOO(2)	1862*	514	Denny	IP	Built 1853 for Glasgow/Belfast. Operated in 1862/64 on Harwich/Rotterdam service. 1877 Collision/sunk. Raised & Broken up.
112.VELOCITY	1862*	259	Hull	IS	Built 1857 scrapped c1877.
113.EARL of ABERDEEN	1863*	820	Napier,Glasgow	IP	Built 1847 Broken up 1880.
114.HAMBURG	1863*	439	Gourlay	IS	Built 1857 for Dundee,Perth & London S.S. Co. Ltd 6.11.1886 - Sold for scrap.
115.FORTH	1863*	401	Barclay	IS	Built 1855 Stranded in 1876.
116.HERON	1864*	624	Dumbarton	IS	Built 1860 Broken up in 1889.
117.MAAS	1864	692	Northfleet	IP	Broken up in 1890.
118.MERMAID	1864	745	Palmer	IS	Sold by 1875
119.STORK	1864	843	Gourlay	IS	1897 Sold to J. Constant 9.1898 Stranded.
120.ALFORD	1865*	771	Newcastle	IS	Built 1863 Broken up in 1893.
121.ORION	1865	777	Stothert,Bristol	IP	Built as CLIFTON. Broken up in 1890.
122.BENBOW	1865	894	Newcastle	IS	Broken up in 1913.
123.EIDER	1866	541	Gourlay	IP	Broken up in 1889.
124.OSTRICH	1866*	624	Dumbarton	IS	Built 1860. Broken up in 1889.
125.FLORENCE	1866*	660	Glasgow	IP	Built 1864. Broken up in 1882.
126.TAURUS	1866	838	Preston Iron Wks	IP	Cattle boat to Continent. Sold in 1892 to City of London. c1911 - B/U.
127.GRANTON	1866	937	Gourlay	IS	London/Leith 1912 B/U on Firth of Forth.
128.HOLLANDIA	1867	820	London & Glasgow SB Co.	IP	London/Holland Broken up 1888
129.HILDA	1868*	428	Samuelson,Hull	IP	Built 1862 as EUGENIE for S. Eastern Railway Company. Renamed CORNUBIA in 1863. Purchased in 1868 and renamed HILDA for excursions to Margate and Ramsgate. Broken up in 1889.
130.LIBRA	1869	1030	Gourlay	IS	London/Hamburg. 1889 Collision/sunk.
131.SCORPIO	1869	885	Palmer	IS	Deleted by 1875
132.VIRGO	1870	1016	Gourlay	IS	London/Hamburg Broken up in 1927.
133.RAINBOW(2)	1871	1083	Gourlay	IS	London/Bordeaux. 1902 Sold McDowall & Barbour ren. MARGARITA later owned by New Hellenique McDowall, Greece. 27.11.1916 -Torpedoed & sunk in Eastern Med.

Name	Date Acquired * or Built	Grt	Builder	Type	Career
134.IRIS	1872	1033	Lewis & Stockwell	IS	London/Hamburg 1914 - Detained at Hamburg 1917 - Sunk in Gulf of Pernau
135.HOBOKEN	1873	413	Napier, Glasgow	IP	Built 1873 as Elbe tender for Adler Line, purchased 1877. Broken up in 1897.
136.CAPULET	1874	336	Softley, S/Shields.	IS	Broken up in 10.1903.
137.NAUTILUS	1874	718	Gulston, Sunderland	IS	1914/18 Guardship at Harwich 1.1923 Collision/sunk.
138.THE PRINCESS	1874	510	Cleland,Tyne	IS	Chartered from D.Reid,Newcastle
139.CONDOR	1875	682	Gourlay	IS	6.1906 Sold for scrap to J.J. King
140.CURLEW	1875	630	Gourlay	IS	2.1896 Wrecked.
141.MARTIN	1875	959	Mitchell	IS	1897 Sold to C. Wilkinson,London then to Spanish owner. c1905 - Broken up.
142.MERLIN	1875	643	Hall,Russell	IS	1.1911 Wrecked.
143.PLOVER	1875	949	Mounsey & Foster	IS	Broken up in 1929.
144.SWALLOW	1875	625	Pearce, Stockton	IP	London/Ostend to 1901 Broken up in 1901.
145.SWIFT	1875	625	Pearce, Stockton	IP	London/Ostend to 1901 1901 Sold to J.Power & Co. Broken up 1902 in Holland.
146.TERN	1875	959	Gourlay	IS	3.1931 Collision/sunk in Humber.
147.FALCON	1876	649	Mitchell	IS	1919 - Made 1st company voyage to Hamburg after WWI. 10.1926 - Fire/lost.
148.HAWK	1876	648	Gourlay	IS	2.1897 Stranded & condemned.
149.PENGUIN	1876	906	Gourlay	IS	13.2.1889 Fire/sank North Sea.
150.PETREL	1876	841	Hall,Russell	IS	7.1912 Collision/sunk.
151.TEAL	1876	830	Pearse	IS	29.4.1916 - War loss.
152.WIDGEON	1876	788	Mitchell	IS	12.1911 Collision & later B/U.
153.OSPREY	1877	1095	Pearse	IS	6.1904 Collision/sunk.
154.KESTREL	1878	956	Gourlay	IS	2.1893 Collision/sunk in Elbe.
155.BITTERN	1878	947	Pearse	IS	1900 Sold to Cia Trasmediterranea Spain ren. VICENTE FERRER. Broken up c1927.
156.GANNET	1879	1127	Pearse	IS	7.7.1916 - War loss
157.LAPWING	1879	1215	Gourlay	IS	1911 Sold & ren. AZIZ (Tu) later SAHIR (Tu) Broken up c 1925.
158.ARDANBHAN	1880	1132	Murray	IS	1880 - Sold to McLaren,Crum 1887 - Sold to Clark & Service 2.1900 - Wrecked.
159.REDSTART	1880	904	Pearse	IS	1914/18 - Guardship at Harwich 1931 Sold LEON MOREAU (Fr) 1932 - Broken up.

Name	Date Acquired * or Built	Grt	Builder	Type	Career
160.DEAK/SWAN	1880	1231	Blackwood & Gordon		Purchased 1882 ren. SWAN 1st company ship built of steel 1904 Sold & ren. ELENA D (Ru) 1924 - B/U at Odessa.
161.CORMORANT	1882	927	W. Walker	IS	Broken up in 1926.
162.MALLARD	1882	1250	Gourlay	IS	1926 Sold to Palgrave,Murphy ren. CITY OF DUBLIN. 8.1948 B/U at Dublin.
163.RAVEN	1883	1648	Pearse	IS	Broken up in 1914.

N.B. ALL SHIPS FROM HERE EXCEPT Nos 173,180,187,188,189,190,191 & 202 ARE BUILT OF STEEL

Name	Date Acquired * or Built	Grt	Builder	Career
164.CYGNET	1883	2012	Gourlay	12.1903 Lost by explosion & fire in cargo 60 miles S of Vigo.
165.ALBATROSS	1884	1450	Palmer	1923 Sold & ren. RACHEL (It) 1924 - Broken up.
166.EGRET	1883	696	Armstrong, Mitchell	1903 Sold to C. Hannevig, Horten ren. ELFI (No) c1906 - Broken up.
167.GREBE	1887	761	Gourlay	1925 - Sold to Italian owners ren. ORSOLA CASUBOLO later CITTA DI BARLETTA, and ANNA ZIPPITELLI. 5.11.1941 - War loss.
168.HALCYON	1887	553	J.Scott, Kinghorn	Thames & coastal paddler 1904 Sold to South of England Steamb 1906 Repurchased & sold to Hamburg Stade-Atlander-Linie ren. CUXHAVE used as a river boat on the Elbe.
169.STARLING	1887	804	Palmer	7.3.1918 - Collision/sunk 7 miles W o Treport o.v. London/Bordeaux.
170.MAVIS	1888	537	J.Scott, Kinghorn	Thames & coastal paddler 1910 - Sold to Pockett's Bristol Chann S.P. Co. Ltd. 1915 - Broken up at Briton Ferry.
171.ORIOLE	1888	643	J.Scott, Kinghorn	Thames & coastal paddler 1912 - Sold to Holland and reduced to hulk.
172.SEAMEW	1888	1543	Palmer	London/Leith service 1914 - DAFNI (Gr) 12.1923-Broken

Name	Date Acquired * or Built	Grt	Builder	Career
173.HERON(2)	1889	879	Gourlay	30.9.1917 - War loss
174.LAVEROCK	1889	544	J.Scott, Kinghorn	Thames & coastal paddler 1908 - Sold to Cie Maritime Bordeaux-Ocean,Bordeaux ren. VILLE DE ROYAN 1922 - Broken up.
175.PHILOMEL	1889	662	J.Scott, Kinghorn	Thames & coastal paddler 1907 - Sold to Furness Railway Barrow - Fleetwood service. 11.1913 - Broken up at Barrow
176.HIRONDELLE	1890	1607	Gourlay	London/Bordeaux service 25.4.1917 - War loss
177.PTARMIGAN	1891	780	Gourlay	15.4.1915 - War loss.
178.PEREGRINE	1891	1664	W.B. Thompson Dundee	1891 - Sold to Howard Smith,Australia. 1916 - Sold to Moller,Shanghai 15.6.1917 - Stranded at Portland Bill 7.1917 - Refloated & towed to S.Wales 1919 - Admiralty storage hulk on the Medway. 20.3.1922 - Sold B/U in Germany.
179.LINNET	1892*	1770	Campbeltown	1890 Built as DIEPPOIS (Fr) 8.1901 Damaged by fire & sold to Uruguayan owner ren. LINO. 1910 - SANDIS 1911 - MICHAEL A.ANDRITSAKIS WWI war loss.
180.PEREGRINE(2)	1892	1681	W.B. Thompson Dundee	Harwich/Hamburg service 1914 - Flotilla supply ship 1915 - Returned to GSNC 29.12.1917 - Wrecked nr Sunk L.V o.v. Rotterdam/Harwich.
181.SPARROW	1892	395	J.F. Meursing, Amsterdam	Purchased on the stocks 6.1894 Sold to African SS Co. for W. African local service. 13.8.1894 - Wrecked on Lagos Bar.
182.ADJUTANT	1893	2394	W. Gray	22.10.1914 - Collision with OCEAN PRINCE of Prince Line & sank off Deal o.v. Naples/London.
183.GUILLIEMOT	1894	1771	Campbeltown	12.1911 - Foundered.

Name	Date Acquired * or Built	Grt	Builder	Career
184.TETUAN	1898*	1394	J.Scott, Kinghorn	Built 1896 1900 - Sold & ren. DANIA (Sw) WWI war loss.
185.EAGLE(3)	1898	647	Gourlay	1928 - Sold for breaking up.
186.SHELDRAKE	1898*	2697	Osborne,Graham	Built 1894 as KELVINGROVE 8.11.1916 - War loss.
187.PRESTON	1899*	2099	Pearce	Built 1885 for Ropner. 2.5.1906 - Wrecked at Point Bay near Camarinas o.v. London/Genoa with general cargo.
188.AUK	1899*	1055	E. Withy	Built 1877 as TINTERN ABBEY for Pyman,Watson & Co. Ltd. 8.1915 - Sunk at Hamburg.
189.VESUVIO	1900*	1391	Laing	Built 1879 as CZAR for Ben Line 12.1898 - Sold to Mossgiel SS Co. Ltd, Glasgow ren. VESUVIO. 6.4.1916 - War loss.
190.BALGOWNIE	1901*	1061	A. Hall	Built 1880 for Grampian SS Co. Ltd 6.2.1916 - War loss.
191.MERANNIO	1901*	1455	W. Gray	Built 1881. Purchased 1901 from. Maclay & McIntyre,Glasgow. Sold 1930 to Palgrave,Murphy ren. CITY OF CORK. 38 - BUTE (Br) 39 - PARITA (Gr) 23.8.1939 - Run aground at Tel Aviv while carrying refugees.
192.PEARL	1901	191	J.P. Rennoldson	27 - HURSLEY (C.V. Hardy,Hull) Broken up c1930.
193.ALOUETTE	1901*	570	Denny	Built 1894 as CALVADOS for London,Brighton & S.Coast Railway London/Ostend service for GSNC. 1924 - Broken up at Rainham.
194.GRONINGEN	1902	988	Raylton Dixon	23.9.1915 - War loss.
195.SWIFT(2)	1902*	671	Sunderland SB	Built in 1884. P'ch's'd from Hull & Netherlands SS Co 1911 - Sold to Bank of Athens, ren. OSMANIE (A. Gaetano & Co,mgr) 1933 - Broken up.

Name	Date Acquired * or Built	Grt	Builder	Career
196.ORTOLAN	1902	1917	Caledon	14.6.1917 - War loss.
197.BULLFINCH	1903	246	Selby SB	27 - ARCHMOR (Br) Survived WWII, trace lost.
198.GOLDFINCH	1903	246	Selby SB	27 - SONNIA (Br) Broken up c1930.
199.LEEUWARDEN	1903	990	Raylton Dixon	17.3.1915 - War loss.
200.CRANE	1904	2033	Ropner	1930 - Sold & ren. KOTOR (Yu) 1934 - Broken up.
201.STORK(2)	1904	2029	Ropner	29.3.1936 - Arr. Blyth B/U.
202.JEANIE HOPE	1905*	105	Hawthorns,Leith	Iron screw dandy. Built 1881 as ANNIE HOPE. Sold & ren. LYD (Br)
203.GRIVE	1905	2037	Caledon	8.12.1917 - Torpedoed off Lerwick, foundered 16 days later.
204.KELVINSIDE	1906*	219	Scott & Co, Bowling	Built 1893 as HARE. Purchased as KELVINSIDE from J.Crisp & Son, Gt. Yarmouth. 1922 Sold to A. Dempsey,London 1933 - Broken up.
205.KINGFISHER	1906	982	Denny	Thames & coastal excursions 1912 - Sold to Tripovich & Co ren. VENEZIA for Trieste/Venice run. 1913 - Converted to oil fuel burning. 20 - Sold to China New Era Shpg. Co. of Hong Kong, name unchanged. Presumed B/U c1937.
206.WOODCOCK	1906	1673	Gourlay	London/Leith 1926 - Sold & ren. OTRANTO (It) 20.3.1934 - Foundered off N. Luzon o.v. Venice/Shanghai.
207.DRAKE	1908	2267	Ailsa	Ren. WILDRAKE 11.14-DRAKE 30.9.1917 - War loss as DRAKE.
208.GOLDEN EAGLE	1909	793	J. Brown	Thames & coastal excursion paddler Dunkirk evacuation in 1940 1951 - Broken up at Grays,Essex.
209.LAVEROCK(2)	1909	1199	Ailsa	38 - Sold to Verano SS Co. Ltd, Gibraltar ren. BELLEROCK

Name	Date Acquired * or Built	Grt	Builder	Career
				15.7.1940 - Mined/sunk in Bristol Channel o.v. Barry to Corunna with coal, 17 lost.
210.CORNCRAKE	1910	1179	Ailsa	37 - CHLORIS (M-H) 1.9.1945 - On fire & submerged at Trieste. 6.1946 - Raised by Italians and returned to service as SARGA. (S.a.r.g.a., Genoa) 1953 - Deleted.
211.LAPWING(2)	1911	1192	Mackie & Thomson	11.11.1917 - War loss.
212.SWIFT(3)	1911	1141	Ramage & Ferguson	1914 - DEAN SWIFT before returning to SWIFT again in 1919. 1929 Sold to Aberdeen S.N. Co. Ltd ren. HARLAW. 46 - MIN CHIH (Chinese) 47 - HAI YANG 49 - CHEPO 50 - HOLLINA 53 - EL BRENON 59 - TRIUMPH 28.8.1963 - Arrived at Hong Kong for breaking up.
211.FAUVETTE	1912	2644	Raylton Dixon	9.3.1916 - War loss.
214.KINGFISHER(2)	1913	289	G. Brown	10.1931 - Damaged by collision & towed into port. Total loss & B/U.
215.ORIOLE(2)	1914	1489	Ailsa	30.1.1915 - War loss.
216.RAVEN(2)	1914	1337	Ailsa	5.1930 - Collision/sunk.
217.SEAMEW(2)	1915	1332	Ailsa	38 - CAVEROCK 47 - CITY OF ANTWERP 53 - Broken up at Dublin.
218.HALCYON(2)	1915	1319	Ailsa	7.4.1916 - War loss.
219.HERO	1916*	771	Earle	Built 1895 for Wilson Line,Hull. 1906 - To Wilson's & N.E. Railway 1916 - Purchased & chartered to Ellerman 1923/26. 1933 - Broken up.
220.PHILOMEL(2)	1917	3050	Ailsa	16.9.1918 - War loss.

Name	Date Acquired * or Built	Grt	Builder	Career
221.HERON(3)	1920	1314	Ailsa	35- BALTEAKO (United Baltic SS) 29.3.1946 - Struck submerged object to N of Fehman Islands o.v. London/ Gydnia. Capsized & sank.
222.STARLING(2)	1920	1303	Ailsa	30 - BALTALLINN(United Baltic SS) 20.9.1941 - War loss.
223.PETREL(2)	1920	1457	Ailsa	26.9.1941 - War loss.
224.LAPWING(3)	1920	1443	Bow,McLachlan	26.9.1941 - War loss.
225.HALCYON(3)	1920	1580	Ailsa	34 - ZAMALEK (Eg) Convoy rescue ship during WWII Reverted to Egypt in 1945 11.1956 - Scuttled at Suez.
226.PHILOMEL(3)	1921	1563	Ailsa	34 - ZAAFAREN (Eg) 5.7.1942 - Sunk by aircraft o.v. Glasgow/Rejkjavik/Russia while acting as convoy rescue ship in convoy PQ17.
227.AUK(2)	1921	1445	Bow,McLachlan	27.7.1944 - War loss.
228.GANNET(2)	1921	1443	Bow,McLachlan	12.1953 - Arr. Grays for B/U.
229.TEAL(2)	1921	1444	Bow,McLachlan	39 - PENESTIN (Cie Nantaise) 55 - LE VAN THUONG (Saigon) 7.1.1957 - Wrecked off Culao Re on the Indo-China coast.
230.IRIS(2)	1921	445	J. Crichton	Completed as KINNAIRD HEAD Purchased 1921 1927 - Sold to James Fisher & Sons Ltd ren. LOUGH FISHER. 28.12.1935 Grounded 3m NW of Barrow & sank o.v. Ayr/Barrow with coal.
231.BLACKCOCK	1921	492	Day,Summers	37 - BROOKTOWN 37 - RORA HEAD 39 - To N. Scotland,Orkney & Shetland Shpg. Co. Ltd 57 - To Hay & Co., Lerwick 58 - GASPARE (It) 72 - Broken up at Trapani, Italy
232.MAVIS(2)	1921	500	Ardrossan	Built 1919 as INDEPENDANCE 1929 - Sold to James Fisher & Sons Ltd

Name	Date Acquired * or Built	Grt	Builder	Career
				ren. SOUND FISHER. 37 - Sold to Empreza International deTransports, Buenos Aires ren. GUADAREMA in 1939. 4.3.1949 - Collision/sunk at Santos Bar.
233.ORIOLE(3)	1921	488	J. Lewis	38 - CANTICK HEAD (A.F. Henry & MacGregor) 55 - BANNSPUR (S.W. Coe) 8.10.1960 - Arr. Dublin for B/U.
234.PTARMIGAN(2)	1921*	499	Ardrossan	Built 1920 as GLANTON FIRTH 38 - ASSUAN 17.10.1943 - Captured/sunk to S.E. of Longstone.
235.DRAKE(2)	1922	1597	Ailsa	34 - AL SAID (Govt. of Zanzibar) 11.8.1956 - Arr. H/Kong for B/U in tow of tug TRADESMAN.
236.GUILLIEMOT(2)	1922*	1909	Tecklenborg	Built 1900 as RAJABURI Purchased as CHAO CHOW FU 1929 - Broken up.
237.SHELDRAKE(2)	1922*	462	Colby Bros	Built 1920 as GLANMOR for Glanmor Shipping Co. Ltd. 37 - STANCREST (J.Billmeir) 27.2.1937 - Missing o.v. London to Bridgwater with cement.
238.ORTOLAN(2)	1923*	489	J. Lewis	Built 1920 as BEAULY FIRTH 50 - BANNTRADER 8.1962 - Broken up at Preston.
239.PERONNE	1923*	207	W.J. Yarwood	Built 1917 1933 - Transfer to Gt. Yarmouth Shpg. Co. Ltd name unchanged 46 - TAYBUOY (Tay Sand Co) Dundee sand dredger 4.6.1960 - Arr. Rosyth for B/U.
240.PICARDY	1923*	320	Crabtree	Built 1920 1931 - Transfer to Gt. Yarmouth Shpg. Co.Ltd name unchanged. 53 - EDITH (Barlow & Co,Dundee) 1.1966 - B/U at St. Davids on Forth.

Name	Date Acquired * or Built	Grt	Builder	Career
241.PEREGRINE(3)	1924*	933	Hawthorns,Leith	Built 1921 as ARBONNE 38 - ARBEL (Be) 12.4.1941 - Bombed/sunk off Cornwall o.v. Maryport/Plymouth with coal. 3 lost.
242.ADJUTANT(2)	1924*	1942	Grangemouth	Built 1922 as MYRTLEPARK 50 - DEVONBROOK 51 - MATHEUS (Fi) 61 - REVENCA (It) 27.2.1964 - Stranded off Istria o.v. Port Said to Portorosa with salt, refloated & B/U at Trieste.
243.ALOUETTE(2)	1924*	638	Ardrossan	Built 1920 as PENTLAND FIRTH 36 - DUNVEGAN HEAD 22.6.1944 - Sunk at Normandy.
244.FAUVETTE(2)	1924*	429	Aitken & Mansel	Built 1874 as HONFLEUR for London & S.W. Railway Co. 12 - CHRYSSELIS (Gr) 16 - CRYSALIS (Fr) 24 - Purchased & ren. FAUVETTE 25 - IHSANIE (Tu) 26 - AIDIN (Tu) 27 - AYDIN (Tu) 33 - CIHAT (Tu) 38- DEMIRHISAR(Tu) 86 - RAHMI KAPTAN (Tu) 1999 - Still trading at 125 years old !
245. ALBATROSS(2)	1924	1942	GRANGE	1939 - Sold to Atlantic & Med. Trading Co. Ltd, London ren. ATLANTIC GUIDE. 27.5.1940 - Sunk as a blockship at Zeebrugge.
246.CRESTED EAGLE	1925	1078	J. S. White	29.5.1940 - War loss.
247.ROEK	1925	1041	Ailsa	12.5.1940 - War loss.
248.MEREL	1925	1088	Ayrshire Dkyd	8.12.1939 - War loss.
249.FAUVETTE(3)	1925	890	J. S. White	25.10.1934 - Sunk in collision in North Sea o.v. Antwerp/London.
250.HIRONDELLE(2)	1925	893	Greenock Dyyd	48 - LANDES (M-H) See MH23.

Name	Date Acquired * or Built	Grt	Builder	Career
251.GREBE(2)	1926	880	Ailsa	37 - PHILOTIS (M-H) 3.9.1940 - War loss.
252.NERO	1927*	640	Harkess	Built 1907 as TRUTHFUL 07 - SUSSEX COAST 14 - WIRRAL COAST 16 - CLADDAGH 24 - NERO (Ellerman Wilson Line) 10.1927 - Purchased by GSNC 11.1927 - Sold back to Ellerman W. 28 - CRISTINA (It) 29 - GAGLIARDO (It) 31 - IMOLA (It) 33 - MARCHIGIANO (It) 13.3.1936 - Explosion/sunk in Red Sea, 7 lost.
253.WOODCOCK(2)	1927	1827	Grangemouth	39 - LORMONT (M-H) See MH18
254.FALCON(2)	1927	1316	Ailsa	28.3.1957 - Arr. Bo'ness B/u.
255.CORMORANT(2)	1927	1220	Earle's	27.6.1957 - Arr. Grays for B/U.
256.YELLOWHAMMER	1928	217	Crabtree	Built 1928 as ROBIN. Ren. in 1929 33 - Transfer to Gt. Yarmouth Shpg. Co.Ltd name unchanged 48 - LINDEAN 53 - BIBE 75 - NOMAD 77 - LINDEAN 92 - Vessel deleted from register as existence in doubt.
257.SILVERTHORN	1928*	436	Wood,Skinner	Built 1908 as DEUX FRERES Transfer from Bennett SS Co. Ltd 37 - Sold to S. W. Coe,Liverpool Broken up in 1952.
258.GRONINGEN(2)	1928	1202	Ailsa	58 - Ren. PHILOMEL (5) 25.5.1961 - Arr. Grays B/U.
259.WOODLARK	1928	1501	Ailsa	54 - HALCYON MED 56 - ASHA 1967 - Broken up in India.
260.LEEUWARDEN(2)	1929	1209	Ailsa	24.2.1946 - Mined & lost.

Name	Date Acquired * or Built	Grt	Builder	Career
261.GOLDFINCH(2)	1929*	327	W.J. Yarwood	Built 1927 as VIVONIA 33 - Transfer to Gt. Yarmouth Shpg. Co. Ltd name unchanged 36 - Ren. LYNN TRADER See GY3
262.ROYAL SOVEREIGN(2)	1929*	891	Fairfield	Twin-funnelled Thames paddler Built 1893 for New Palace Steamers Ltd for London/Margate/Ramsgate. 3.1929 - Purchased 2.1930 B/U in Holland.
263.STARLING(3)	1930	1320	Ailsa	8.1960 - Arrived Grays,Essex for Breaking up.
264.MAVIS(3)	1930	935	Workman,Clark	20.5.1940 - War loss.
265.SWIFT(4)	1930	936	Workman,Clark	48 - LORMONT (M-H) See MH24
266.ROYAL EAGLE	1932	1532	Cammell,Laird	Excursion paddle steamer Withdrawn at end 1950 season. 54-Broken up after layup in Medway
267.TERN(2)	1932	213	J.Koster	1st company motor vessel 49 - HINDLEA 52 - GEORGE EMELIE 60 - HENNING MATHIESEN 60 - Converted to suction dredger 65 - ANDERS MARTIN 68 - MARTIN 68 - DAMMANN 72 - KNUD DAMMANN 75 - BURGUNDIA 2.1989 - Suffered severe heavy weather damage, scuttled 3.1989.
268.VOLGA	1932*	281	McIlwaine & Lewis	Built 1881 as TOPIC for Belfast S.S. Co. Ltd Transfer from Bennett S.S. Co. Ltd 5.1937 - Broken up at Bo'ness.
269.CONIFER	1932*	453	J. Crichton	Built 1920 as EGHAM Transfer from London & Dunkirk Shpg.Co. Ltd Broken up c1937.
270.ISLE of ARRAN	1933*	313	T.B. Seath	Built 1892 for Buchanan Steamers Ltd Paddler for excursions & PLA cruises 10.1936 - Sold for breaking up.

Name	Date Acquired * or Built	Grt	Builder	Career
271.FAUVETTE(4)	1935	614	Furness SB	63 - SOUTHERN STAR 69 - ISLAND SUPPLIER 91 - Deleted from register.
272.LAGUNA BELLE	1935*	617	Denny	Built 1896 for Belle Steamers Ltd as SOUTHEND BELLE. Paddler for excursions & PLA dock cruises. 1939 - Sold to Admiralty 1946 - Broken up.
273.QUEEN of theCHANNEL	1936*	1162	Denny	28.5.1940 - War loss at Dunkirk.
274.PHILOMEL(4)	1936	2122	Caledon	57 - Sold to F.Italo Croce ren. CROCE GUISEPPE (It) 64 - ANESIS (It) 15.2.1967 - Aground 15m E of Lagos o.v. Duala to Spain/Beirut, total loss.
275.MALLARD(2)	1936	352	Caledon	10.7.1940 - War loss.
276.PLOVER(2)	1936	352	Caledon	60 - Transfer to Gt. Yarmouth Shpg. Co. Ltd. name unchanged. 7.11.1961 - Collision/sank in New Waterway, refloated three days later 12.1961 - Arr. Hendrik Ido Ambacht for breaking up.
277.BULLFINCH(2)	1936	433	Caledon	63 - NORMAN COMMODORE 65 - EVANGELISTRIA (Gr) 4.1985 - Broken up at Perama.
278.GOLDFINCH(3)	1937	433	Caledon	62 - ALLEN COMMODORE 66 - THEODOROS (Gr) 76 - STAMATA II (Gr) 12.1984 - Broken up at Eleusis.
279.CRANE(2)	1937	785	Ailsa	64 - NISSOS SIFNOS (Gr) 69 - TOULA (Gr) 75 - AL MADANI (Kuwait) 9.1979 - Laid-up at Kuwait 3.1980 - Aground at Kuwait 81 - GULF ACE 82 - Broken up.
280.STORK(3)	1937	787	Ailsa	23.8.1941 - War loss.
281.HERON(4)	1937	2374	Caledon	56 - KUFRA (M-H) 59 - ARDEN

Name	Date Acquired * or Built	Grt	Builder	Career
				65 - SANMICHAEL (Gr) 73 - GRAND MICHAEL (Cy) 9.1974 - Broken up at Split.
282.ROYAL SOVEREIGN(3)	1937	1527	Denny	9.12.1940 - War loss
283.KINGFISHER(3)	1938	278	J. Koster	24.6.1940 - War loss.
284.ALOUETTE(3)	1938	278	J. Koster	66 - OLYMPOS (Gr) 7.1982 - Broken up at Katakolon in Greece.
285.DRAKE(3)	1938	531	J. Koster	66 - CHRISTOS II (Gr) 77 - DEMETRA I (Cy) 79 - TINOS 91 - Deleted from Register.
286.ROYAL DAFFODIL	1939	2060	Denny	1.2.1967 - Arr. Ghent B/U.
287.ORIOLE(4)	1939	489	H. Robb	62 - L'ORIOLE (Can) 64 - CECILIENNE MARIE 67 - CECILIENNE 70 - MARINE TRADER 83 - MAYAN TRADER 87 - GONAIVES TRADER 87 - N.D. LOURDES 88 - NOTRE DAME de LOURDES 1.1.1991 - Took water & sank off Santo Domingo Cay, Bahamas o.v. Miami to Gonaives (Haiti) 5 lost.
288.WEST COASTER/ MALLARD(4)	1943*	361	Smit & Zoon	Built 1938 for Brit. Isles Coasters Ltd 50 - MALLARD 64 - ALLARD (A.R.C. Marine) 9.1984 - Broken up at Gravesend.
289.MALLARD(3)	1944	377	H. Scarr	48 - NORWICH TRADER (Gt. Yarmouth Shpg. Co. Ltd) 65 - NIKOLAOS 1988 - Broken up at Aliaga.
290.LAPWING(4)	1944	921	Goole SB	22.3.1967 - Sustained extensive damage in Collision in Thames. 31.31967 -Arr. at Grays for B/U.
291.KINGFISHER(4)	1944	493	H. Robb	66 - DUNURE (Can) 15.12.1983 Scuttled off St. John's(NF). by owners.

Name	Date Acquired * or Built	Grt	Builder	Career
292.STORK(4)	1945	493	H. Robb	66 - NIKOS LITOCHORON (Gr) 99 - Still in service in Greece.
293.PETREL(3)	1945	921	Goole SB	61 - PETRELL (No) 65 - COSTAKIS S 66 - ANNA 88 - JUNIOR (Ho) & broken up.
294.MAVIS(4)	1946	381	H. Scarr	66 - ATHANASIOS A 70 - LIMNOS 1999 - Still in service.
295.CORNCRAKE(2)	1946	640	H. Robb	67 - TWILLINGATE (Can) 5.1995 - Deleted, lack of information
296.REDSTART(2)	1946	640	H. Robb	67 - KAPTA MATHIOS 69 - SPYROS G 8.2.1977 - Sank off Libya.
297.PEREGRINE(4)	1946*	890	A. & J. Inglis	Built 1940 as EMPIRE SPINNEY 65 - LIBYA 71 - ROZMARY 91 - Deleted from register, vessel's existence in doubt.
298.GREENFINCH	1946*	392	Van Diepen	Blt as CARIBE II in 1940 40 - EMPIRE DAFFODIL 66 - MOIRA 66 - STAR OF MEDINA 91 - Deleted from register, vessel's existence in doubt.
299.WOODWREN	1947*	973	Nuske,Stettin	Built 1912 as BORUSSIA 39 - TIMANDRA 5.45 - Taken as prize at Hamburg 46 - EMPIRE CONFAL 47 - Ren. WOODWREN 53 - ARTEMIS cut down to deck level, used as coal hulk at Gravesend 10.1960 - B/U at Queenborough.
300.RINGDOVE	1947*	958	F. Schicau	Built 1912 as BADENIA 39 - TITANIA 5.1945 - Taken in prize at Rendsburg 46 - EMPIRE CONEXE 47 - Purchased ren. RINGDOVE 50 - Broken up at Bo'ness.

Name	Date Acquired * or Built	Grt	Builder	Career
301.LAVEROCK(3)	1947	1209	S.P. Austin	65 - CHANIA II (Gr) 5.1980 - Broken up at La Spezia.
302.SEAMEW(3)	1947	1209	S.P. Austin	66 - MARIGO 72 - CAPETAN CHRONIS (Gr) 3.6.1974 - Collision/sunk in posn. 34-05N 20-45 E to N of Benghazi.
303.ALBATROSS(3)	1947*	1925	J. Cockerill	Built 1943 as WESERSTROM 45-EMPIRE GALENA 47-ALBATROSS 58-PORT CAPETOWN 59-FRONTIER 66-FORTUNE 12.1968 - B/u H/Kong.
304.SHELDRAKE(3)	1947*	1925	Stettin	Built 1944 as NJONG 45 - EMPIRE GARLAND 47 - SHELDRAKE 59 - SALEMSTAR 60 - AMBELOS (Gr) 61 - MARMINA (Gr) 68 - FILIO (Gr) 6.1972 - B/U in Greece.
305.TEAL(3)	1947	1148	Goole SB	63 - GLENCOE (Can) 87 - JEHOVAH STAR 88 - ETOILE de BETHLEHEM 89 - IRON MAIDEN 99 - Still in service.
306.CRESTED EAGLE	1947*	249	J. Crown	Built 1938 as NEW ROYAL LADY 47 - ROYAL LADY 11.1947 - Purchased for PLA dock cruises 1957 - Sold to Malta ren.IMPERIAL EAGLE and still in use there at Gozo at the Millennium.
307.WOODCOCK(3)	1948	959	Grangemouth	64 - ORJULA (Yu) 6.1984 - Broken up at Rijeka.
308.GREBE(3)	1948	933	H. Robb	18.10.1967 - Arr. Newport for B/U.
309.PTARMIGAN(3)	1948	959	Grangemouth	63 - LABIN 67 - RABAC (Yu) 10.1982 - Broken up at Rijeka.

Name	Date Acquired * or Built	Grt	Builder	Career
310.ROYAL SOVEREIGN(4)	1948	1851	Denny	67 - AUTOCARRIER for Dover/ Zeebrugge freight service,12 passengers(Townsend Thoresen) 74 - ISCHIA (It) 99 - Still in service as ro-ro cargo/ferryowned by Traghetti Pozzuoli, Naples.
311.ROBIN REDBREAST	1949*	157	J. Harker	Tank barge built 1930 as CONSTANCE H for John Harker Ltd, Knottingly.
312.AUK(3)	1949	1238	S.P. Austin	65 - OURANOPOLIS (Gr) 1993 - Hulked in the Bitter Lakes,Egypt.
313.QUEEN of theCHANNEL (2)	1949	1472	Denny	68 - OIA (Gr) 13.9.1974 - Arr. Perama leaking, laid-up & later scrapped.
314.HIRONDELLE (3)	1950	757	H. Robb	66 - CLYDE (Can) 93 - Towed Sydney(CB) - Halifax & donated to Royal Canadian Navy as target practice.
315.SWIFT(5)	1950	757	H. Robb	67 - CIKAT (Yu) 78 - UNITY (Cy) 23.5.1982 - Foundered S of Cyprus in position 34-20 N 32-33 E.
316.ORTOLAN(3)	1951*	522	Goole SB & E	1945 Built as EMPIRE SEABRIGHT 49 - HELEN SEABRIGHT 51 - ORTOLAN 58 - GEORGIOS K (Gr) 62 - LAUT MAS (Sg) 64 - PASTEUR 14.1.1971 - Sank near Alida Shoal, 180 miles to E of Singapore o.v. Sibu/Singapore.
317. GULL	1952	75	J.R. Hepworth, Paull	Motor Tug Sold & later ren. NIPAROUND
318.TERN(3)	1953	1028	Cook,Welton & Gemmell	64 - AVRA 70 - ARGYRO 74 - DEBORAH I

Name	Date Acquired * or Built	Grt	Builder	Career
				91 - Deleted due to absence of reports, continued existence in doubt.
319.WHITEWING	1953	1102	Ailsa	64 - ORUDA (Yu) 6.1983 - Broken up at Rijeka.
320.RINGDOVE(2)	1954	1102	Ailsa	67 - HORIZONT 73 - OTOK (Yu) 12.1983 - Broken up at Split.
321.ADJUTANT(3)	1954	1366	S.P. Austin	66 - GALIOLA (Yu) 1.1983 - Broken up at Split.
322.WOODLARK(2)	1956	933	Grangemouth	69 - LONGMOOR FREIGHTER 71 - MARCHWOOD FREIGHTER 19.5.1979 - Arrived Sittingbourne for breaking up.
323.GANNET(2)	1956	923	Grangemouth	68 - SARAH (Can) 7.11.1984 - Struck wreck & sank in Road Bay,Anguilla during hurricane. Subsequently raised & scuttled.
324.WOODWREN(2)	1956*	968	Gragemouth	Built as EDDYSTONE in 1954 69 - LOVRAN (Yu) 7.1988 - Broken up at Split.
325.HERON(5)	1957	943	C. Hill	69 - THELMA P 70 - ANASTASIA 12.73 - Disappeared o.v. Piraeus to Livorno.
326.SANDPIPER	1957	916	H. Robb	67 - ILE de SAINTE PIERRE (Can) 81 - ALINDA 82 - KATIA K 89 - VOYAGER II 4.1989 - Broken up at Gadani Beach.
327. SWALLOW(2)	1961*	1463	Aalborg	Built as DORRIT CLAUSEN 49 - TEXELSTROOM 61 - SWALLOW 67 - EVILPIS 13.1.1968 - Sank off Navarino Bay after developing engine trouble during heavy weather o.v. Benghazi to Ravenna. All crew of 16 lost.

Name	Date Acquired * or Built	Grt	Builder	Career
328.PHILOMEL(6)	1961*	1662	A.G. Weser	Built as MANCHESTER VENTURE in 1956 at Bremerhaven. 61 - PHILOMEL 68 - BAT TIRAN 8.1972 - Beached after explosion & fire in cargo o.v. Rijeka to Haifa. 12.9.1972 - Arr. Piraeus for B/U.
329. SHELDRAKE(4)	1963*	1662	A.G. Weser	Built as MANCHESTER VANGUARD in 1956 at Bremerhaven. 1959 - First vessel into the St. Lawrence Seaway. 63 - SHELDRAKE 68 - BAT GOLAN 74 - WOOCHUCK 75 - SELATAN MAJU 82 - WIHAR I 5.1985 - Broken up at Hong Kong.
330.ORIOLE(5)	1963	430	J. Lewis	77 - JUDERT (Pa) 82 - JUDERT II (Pa) 4.3.1983 - Sank off Collo, Algeria in position 37-38 N 6-39 E following a collision and sustaining hull cracks.
331.ORTOLAN(4)	1964	430	J. Lewis	79 - MARAL R 26.8.1987 - Aground at Seaton Sluice, Northumberland having sailed from Berwick and drifted down coast on fire. Later broken up in situ.
332.ALBATROSS(4)	1965	654	J. Lewis	76 - LADY JEAN 81 - CLEMENTINE 91 - ABAD 92 - ELONA 93 - ORESTIS 96 - ENA 98 - ALATRO 98 - MICHEL I 98 - DISTA 99 - Still in service.
333.AVOCET	1965	654	J. Lewis	76 - AFRODITI H (Cy) 82 - SAMARA 85 - HAMADA 28.6.1993 - Struck submerged object o Ras Banas, Egypt o.v. Jeddah to Suez. Foundered the next day.

Name	Date Acquired * or Built	Grt	Builder	Career
34.PETREL(4)	1965	496	J. Bolson	78 - LATONA (Pa) 99 - Still in service.
35.PLOVER(3)	1965	496	J. Bolson	71 - BEN VEEN Ramsey SS 85 - MEDINA D (Br) 18.10.1988 - Adrift off Suffolk coast, struck submerged object, capsized & sank off East Holm buoy o.v. Rouen to Gt.Yarmouth.
36. TANMERACK	1967	1598	AILSA	Built for Charter Shipping Co. Ltd, a P. & O. subsidiary but crewed & managed by General Steam for a Canadian timber charter to Canadian Pacific. 10.1971 - To P.& O.Short Sea Shipping Ltd 73 - Sold to Coe Metcalf Ltd renamed QUICKTHORN. 90 - AMENCIDA 93 - BIBA 97 - NAHLA Still trading in 1999. N.B. Other company ships were used occasionally on summer charter between the St. Lawrence and Hudson's Bay in post-WWII years including:- SHELDRAKE of 1944 TEAL of 1947 LAVEROCK of 1947 WOODCOCK of 1948 SANDPIPER of 1957.

MOSS HUTCHISON LINE
(Taken over 1935)

MH1.ARDENZA	1935*	933/20	Hawthorns, Leith	46 - CORY FREIGHTER (Br) 52 - ATLANTE (Sp) 9.8.1957 - Stranded on French coast, refloated & B/U at Nantes.
MH2.BUSIRIS	1935*	943/29	Ailsa	48 - KYLEGLEN (Monroe) 22.5.1968 - Arr. Dublin for B/U.
MH3.ESNEH	1935*	1931/19	SH	Ex WESTERN COAST 48 - TEFKROS 58 - SHUN ON 5.1959 - B/U at Hong Kong.
MH4.ETRIB	1935*	1943/19	SH	Ex BRITISH COAST 14.6.1942 - Torpedoed/sunk by U522 in N.Atlantic o.v. Cartagena & Gibraltar to Liverpool.
MH5.FENDRIS	1935*	1309/25	INGLIS	50 - ANNEMARIE KRUGER 9.1959 - B/U at Hamburg.
MH6.HATASU	1935*	3198/21	J. Blumer	2.10.1941 - War loss.
MH7.KANA	1935*	2743/29	MacMillan	52 - TERESA VIGO 60 - MARIA PIRO 65 - OLD OAK 5.1968 - B/U at Trieste.
MH8.KANTARA	1935*	3237/25	BC	22.2.1941 - Sunk by GNEISENAU.
MH9.KAVAK	1935*	2743/29	MacMillan	2.10.1940 - Torpedoed/sunk by U101 in position 55 N 19-30 W.
MH10.KHETI	1935*	2650/27	H & W(Gk)	51 - ALCORA 58 - GAY MED (Le) 64 - MED STAR 9.10.1967 - Sank 20 m S of Pantellaria
MH11.KUFRA	1935*	2608/29	H & W (G)	23.6.1940 - Collision/sunk 60 miles NW of Bayonne o.v. Bordeaux to Bayonne on Admiralty service.
MH12.KYRENIA	1935*	2486/25	BC	Ex NIGERIAN (United Africa) Purchased 1935 37 - TORONTO CITY 1940 - Weather ship in N.Atlantic

Name	Date Acquired * or Built	Grt	Builder	Career
				2.7.1941 - Torpedoed/sunk by U108 in position 27 - 03N 30 W,no survivors
MH13.MEMPHIS	1935*	784/17	ARD	Ex SMERDIS 1938 - CAID-KEBIR (Morocco) 54 - MEZIANE 59 - Deleted from register.
MH14.MEROE	1935*	3832/28	BC	Ex LAFIAN (United Africa) 35 - Purchased by Moss Hutchison 50 - ADELE (Ge) 57 - TUCANA (Ge) 58 - URSULA (Ge) 60 - MIENAN (Pa) 61 - RUHAMAH (H/Kong) 65 - LIBY 68 - B/U in Far East.
MH15.PROCRIS	1935*	1008/24	INGLIS	Broken up end 1950.
MH16.SARDIS	1935*	978/28	ARD	54 - MARICHU 65 - PHLOISVOS 66 - CAPO PALA 67 - AGIOS NICOLAOS 70 - Deleted from register.
MH17.CHLORIS	1937*	1180/10	Ailsa	Ex CORNCRAKE of 1910 1.9.1945 War loss in Mediterranean Subsequently raised by Italians and renamed SARGA, Owned by S.a.r.g.a., Genoa 1953 - Deleted.
MH18.LORMONT	1939*	1561/27	Grangemouth	Ex WOODCOCK of 1927 7.12.1940 - Collision/sunk off Humber while acting as guardship.
MH19.PHILOTIS	1937*	880/26	Ailsa	Ex GREBE of 1926 3.9.1940 - Collision/sunk 8m NW of St. Govens L.V. o.v. Swansea/Lisbon.
MH20.MEMPHIS(2)	1947	3575/47	W. Pickersgill	72 - ELIAS 7.12.1981 - Demolition began at Gadani Beach.
MH21.KANTARA(2)	1947	3213/47	H & W(B)	71 - CONSTANTIS II (Cy) 3.1980 - Sold for B/U in Spain.
MH22.KARNAK	1948	3198/48	H & W(B)	71 - EUDOCIA 28.3.1982 - Dem. began at Bombay

Name	Date Acquired * or Built	Grt	Builder	Career
MH23.LANDES	1948*	893/25	Greenock Dyk	Ex HIRONDELLE of 1925 53 - PILARELLA (It) 58 - TURRITANIA (It) 9.10.1960 - Aground at Gefle in Sweden, sold by auction & 9.6.1961 arrived Lubeck for B/U.
MH24.LORMONT(2)	1948*	936/30	WC	Ex SWIFT of 1930 53 - SILVER MED (Cy) 60 - SILVER KING (Pa) 65 - SOUTH SEA (Pa) 68 - EUGENIE 9.1968 - Sold for B/U H/Kong.
MH25.AMARNA	1949	3422/49	H & W(G)	67 - ASSYRIA (Cunard) 68 - AMARNA 75 - KASTRIANI III (Gr) 84 - Broken up at Gadani Beach.
MH26.ASSIOUT	1949	3422/49	H & W(B)	73 - CHRYSSOULA II 12.1981 - Demolition. began at Gadani Beach.
MH27.KYPROS	1950	3499/50	PICK	67 - AURANIA (Cunard charter) 68 - KYPROS 76 - ANGELIKI 81 - ANGEL 4.1982 - Sold for B/U at Calcutta.
MH28.TABOR	1952	3694/52	CAL	75 - KATIA (Gr) 82 - KATE 3.1982 - Demolition began at Beypore in India.
MH29.KUFRA(2)	1956*	2409/37	CAL	See HERON of 1936
MH30.MELITA	1971	2686/71	HALL	79 - SIBONEY (Pa) 14.6.1987 - Arr. Tampico for breaking up.
MH31.MAKARIA	1972	2686/72	HALL	79 - LOS TEQUES 7.1987 - Demolition began in Mexico.

GRAND UNION SHIPPING CO. LTD.

Name	Date Acquired * or Built	Grt	Builder	Career
GU1. MARSWORTH	1937*	368	J. Smit, Viervelaten	Built as KONINGSDIEP in 1925 Purchased as MERWEDE 49 - Sold ren. BAITARANI 57 - SAVITRI (It) Subsequently broken up in Italy during the 1960s.
GU2. BLISWORTH	1940*	738	AILSA	Built 1902 as KATHLEEN 50 - HOLDERNIDD (Holderness) 11.2.1956 - Arr. Gateshead for B/U.
GU3. KILWORTH	1943*	791	HARKESS	Built as ESKWOOD in 1911 1946 - Ren. KILWORTH 50 - FENCHURCH (Br) 51 - HOLDERNOLL (Br) 20.1.1956 - Arr. Gateshead for B/U.
GU4. BOSWORTH	1946	865	BURNT	19.1.1965 - Wrecked on St. Pierre & Miquelon o.v. Sydney(NS)to Bonavista.
GU5. KNEBWORTH	1946	857	BURNT	64 - DOMINO RUN 79 - MINO 4.1998 - Deleted from register due to lack of information.
GU6. MARSWORTH(2)	1949*	519	C. HILL	Built in 1947 as SOMERSETBROOK 7.1949 - Purchased 26.11.1953 - Collision/sunk in dense fog off Winterton, 10 miles N of Great Yarmouth o.v. London/Stornoway with cement.
GU7. MARSWORTH(3)	1954*	628	J.LEWIS	Built 1952 as BRIER ROSE 65 - Transferred to Gen. Steam 69 - KIMEN (Yu) 97 - Still trading under flag of St.Vincent & Grenadines.
GU9. BLISWORTH(2)	1957	1031	A.HALL	70 - FRANCES B 74 - LEILA 1 (Le) 2.1.1987 - Arrived Tripoli in Lebanon for breaking up.

GREAT YARMOUTH SHIPPING CO. LTD.

	Name	Date Acquired * or Built	Grt	Builder	Career
GY1.	PICARDY	1931*	320	CRABTREE	See No. 240 in Main List
GY2.	PERONNE	1933*	207	CRABTREE	See No. 239 in Main List
GY3.	GOLDFINCH/LYNN TRADER	1933*	327	YARWOOD	Built as VIVONIA in 1927 36 - LYNN TRADER 50 - IMOGEN 1.6.1964 - Arr. Cork for B/U by Haulbowline Industries Ltd.
GY4.	YELLOWHAMMER	1933*	217	CRABTREE	See No. 256 in Main List
GY5.	NORWICH TRADER	1934*	217	COCHRANE	Built 1908 ex ELEMORE, ex ESPERANTO. 6.1.1942 - Mined/sunk in position 51-55N 1-32E.
GY6.	YARMOUTH TRADER	1934*	321	CRABTREE	Built 1920 ex ASHDENE, ex STERTPOINT 46 - BEN JEE 11.1952 - Stranded off Isle of Man 12.1952 - Arr. Bruges for B/U.
GY7.	LOWESTOFT TRADER	1934	380	GOOLE	62 - PONTAC 62 - MILOS 64 - VASSILIOS LITOCHORON 79 - SAN ANTONIO (Cy) 1986 - Deleted from register due to lack of information.
GY8.	BOSTON TRADER	1936	380	GOOLE	9.2.1940 - Damaged by bombing near Blakeney Bell Buoy. 62 - MONROE 64 - ELISE MARIE 66 - SONIA D (J.Davie,Quebec) 72 - VIGNAULT B (Can.) 80 - Deleted from register, presumed broken up in Canada.
GY9.	NORWICH TRADER(2)	1948*	377	H.SCARR	See MALLARD No. 289 in Main List.

Name	Date Acquired * or Built	Grt	Builder	Career
GY10.YARMOUTH TRADER(2)	1950*	945	GOOLE	Built as FRIARGATE in 1946 Purchased & ren. in 1950 59 - PROTOPOROS (Gr) 60 - YEWCROFT 65 - GEORGIOS KONTOS 71 - PANAGHIA 18.10.1971 - Developed leaks 4m S of Cape Gata near Limassol, taken in tow but sank next day.
GY11.LYNN TRADER(2)	1951*	404	GOOLE	Built 1945 as EMPIRE FAIRPLAY 49 - HELEN FAIRPLAY 51 - Purchased & renamed. 60 - Sold to Egypt ren. HAMZA I 5. 1995 - Deleted from register due to lack of information.
GY12. NORFOLK TRADER	1956*	457	D.& J. Boot, Alphen	Ex ARBON 70 - CHRISTOFOROS 76 - PHILLIPOS K 83 - GHADA S 83 - DIANA D 23.11.1983 - Collision/sunk with U.S. Navy landing ship FORT SNELLINE 20 miles off Sidon, 35 miles SW Beirut o.v. Vassiliko to Sidon.
GY13. PLOVER	1960*	352	CALEDON	See No. 276 in Main List
GY14. PEREGRINE	1961*	890	A. & J. Inglis	See No. 297 in Main List

NEW MEDWAY STEAM PACKET CO. LTD.

(Taken over in 1936)

NM1. ESSEX QUEEN	1936*	465	DENNY	Built 1897 as WALTON BELLE Purchased in 1925 & renamed 9.1938 - Withdrawn from service 46 - PRIDE OF DEVON 48 - Laid-up at Southampton 1951 - Broken up.
NM2. MEDWAY QUEEN	1936*	316	AILSA	Built 1924, 980 passengers. 1947 - Returned to service after extensive war service. Last season was 1963, laid-up in East India Dock. In 1966 became Clubhouse on River Medina.

Name	Date Acquired * or Built	Grt	Builder	Career
				Isle of Wight. In 1984 she was towed back to the Medway for preservation.
NM3. QUEEN of KENT	1936*	789	HAM	Built 1916 as HMS ATHERSTONE 27 - QUEEN of KENT 49 - LORNA DOONE Withdrawn at end of 1951 season and broken up.
NM4. QUEEN of SOUTHEND	1936*	522	DENNY	Built 1898 as YARMOUTH BELLE 28 - QUEEN of SOUTHEND 38 - THAMES QUEEN 1947 - Broken up.
NM5. QUEEN of THANET	1936*	792	HAM	Built 1916 as HMS MELTON 27 - QUEEN of THANET 49 - SOLENT QUEEN 4.1951 - Caught fire, withdrawn from service and broken up.
NM6.QUEEN of the CHANNEL	1936*	1162	DENNY	Built in 1935 at Dumbarton 28.5.1940 - War loss at Dunkirk.
NM7. ROYAL DAFFODIL	1936*	465	R.Stephenson, Hebburn	Built 1906 as DAFFODIL for Mersey excursions. 34 - ROYAL DAFFODIL 4.1938 - Arr. Ghent for B/U.
NM8. CITY of ROCHESTER	1936*	235	J. Scott, Kinghorn	Built 1904 for Medway excursions Requisitioned for WWI service 1920 - Resumed service 1938 - Broken up.
NM9. ROYAL SOVEREIGN	1937	1527	DENNY	9.12.1940 - Mined/sunk near Barry o.v. Troon to Penarth.
NM10.ROCHESTER QUEEN	1947*	345	Stockton	Built 1944 as a Landing Craft Later JERSEY QUEEN of Jersey Car Ferries.
NM11.ROYAL SOVEREIGN	1948	1851	DENNY	See No. 310 in Main List
NM12. QUEEN of the CHANNEL	1949	1472	DENNY	See No. 313 in Main List

SHIPBUILDERS CODES

AALBORG	Aalborg Vaerft A/S, Denmark
A. HALL	Alexander Hall & Co. Ltd, Aberdeen
AILSA	Ailsa Shipbuilding Co. Ltd, Troon
ARD	Ardrossan Dockyard Ltd, Ardrossan (owned by Coast Lines)
AUSTIN	S. P. Austin & Son Ltd, Sunderland
AYR	Ayrshire Dockyard Ltd, Irvine
B & G	Blackwood & Gordon, Port Glasgow
BARROW	Naval Construction & Armaments Co. Ltd, Barrow
BC	Barclay, Curle & Co. Ltd, Glasgow
BEARD	W. Beardmore & Co. Ltd, Glasgow
BODEWES	Bodewes Scheeps., Martenshoek, Holland
BOLSON	J. Bolson Ltd, Poole
BOW,McLACHLAN	Bow, McLachlan & Co. Ltd, Paisley
BROWN	John Brown & Co. Ltd, Clydebank
BURNT	Burntisland Shipbuilding Co. Ltd, Burntisland
CAIRD	Caird & Co. Ltd, Greenock
CAL	Caledon Shipbuilding & Engineering Co. Ltd, Dundee
CAMPBELTOWN	Campbeltown Shipbuilding Co. Ltd, Campbeltown
CL	Cammell, Laird & Co. Ltd, Birkenhead
CRABTREE	Crabtree & Co., Great Yarmouth
COCKERILL	J. Cockerill, Belgium
CRICHTON	J. Crichton & Co. Ltd, Connah's Quay
DAY SUMMERS	Day, Summers & Co. Ltd, Southampton
De NOORD	N. V. Indust. Maats De Noord, Alblasserdam, Holland
DEEST	N. V. Scheepswerf Deest, Holland
DENNY	William Denny & Bros. Ltd, Dumbarton
DOBIE	Dobie & Company, Glasgow
DOBSON	W. Dibson & Co. Ltd, Newcastle
DUBLIN DKYD	Dublin Dockyard Ltd
DUTHIE TORRY	J. Duthie & Sons Ltd, Aberdeen
EARLE	Earle's Shipbuilding & Dry Dock Co. Ltd, Hull
FAIRFIELD	Fairfield Shipbuilding & Eng. Co. Ltd, Govan
FORTH	Forth Shipbuilding & Eng. Co. Ltd, Alloa
FULLERTON	John Fullerton & Company, Paisley
FURN	Furness Shipbuilding Co. Ltd, Haverton Hill-on-Tees
G. BROWN	George Brown & Co.(Marine) Ltd, Greenock
GOOLE	Goole Shipbuilding & Eng. Co. Ltd, Goole
GOURLAY	Gourlay Brothers, Dundee
GRANGEMOUTH	Grangemouth Dockyard Ltd, Grangemouth
H & W	Harland & Wolff Ltd, Belfast
H & W(G)	Harland & Wolff Ltd, Govan
HARKER	J. Harker, Knottingly
HALL RUSSELL	Hall, Russell & Co. Ltd, Aberdeen
HARKESS	W. Harkess & Son Ltd, Middlesbrough
HAWTHORNS	Hawthorns & Co., Leith
HEND	D. & W. Henderson & Co. Ltd, Glasgow

HILL	Chas. Hill & Sons Ltd, Bristol
HL	Hawthorn, Leslie & Co. Ltd, Hebburn
HOLLAND	Amsterdam shipbuilders
IJSSELWERF	N. V. Ijsselwerf, Rotterdam
INGLIS	A. & J. Inglis Ltd, Pointhouse, Glasgow
IRVINE	Irvine's Shipbuilding & Dry Dock Co. Ltd, West Hartlepool
J. SCOTT	J. Scott of Kinghorn Ltd, Scotland
J. SMIT	J. Smit, Foxhol, Holland
KOSTER	J. Koster, Groningen, Holland
LARNE	Larne Shipbuilding Co. Ltd, Larne
LEWIS	John Lewis & Sons Ltd, Aberdeen
LIFFEY DKYD	Liffey Dockyard Ltd, Dublin
LONDONDERRY	North of Ireland Shipbuilding Co. Ltd, Londonderry
LYTHAM	Lytham Shipbuilding & Eng. Co. Ltd, Lytham
MACKAY	Mackay Bros., Alloa
MACM	A. MacMillan & Son Ltd, Dumbarton
McILWAINE & McCOLL	McIlwaine & McColl, Belfast
MONTROSE	Montrose Shipbuilding & Eng. Co. Ltd, Montrose
MURDOCH & MURRAY	Murdoch & Murray, Port Glasgow
N & M	Napier & Miller Ltd, Old Kilpatrick near Glasgow
NOORD NED	N.V. Noord-Nederlandsche Scheeps., Groningen
NORTHWICH	Northwich shipyards on the river Weaver
PALMER	Palmers Shipbuilding & Iron Co. Ltd, Jarrow
RAMAGE & FERGUSON	Ramage & Ferguson Ltd, Leith
RAYL	Sir Raylton Dixon & Co. Ltd, Middlesbrough
RENNOLDSON	C. Rennoldson & Company, South Shields
RICKMERS	Rickmers Werft., Bremerhaven
ROBB	Henry Robb Ltd, Leith
RUSS	Russell & Co. Ltd, Port Glasgow
SCARR	Henry Scarr Ltd, Hessle
SD	Smith's Dock Co. Ltd, Middlesbrough
SH	Swan, Hunter & Wigham Richardson Ltd, Wallsend
SHEARER	J. Shearer & Company, Glasgow
SMIT & ZOON	E. J. Smit & Zoon Scheeps. N. V., Westerbroek, Holland
STEPHEN	Alexander Stephen & Sons Ltd, Glasgow
STOCKTON	Teesside Shipbuilders Ltd, Stockton
TERNEUZEN	N. V. Terneuzen Scheeps. Mij., Terneuzen, Holland
THOMSON	J. & G. Thomson, Clydebank, Glasgow
TOWERS	Towers Shipbuilding Co. Ltd, Bristol
TYNE IRON	Tyne Iron Shipbuilding Co. Ltd, Wallsend
VAN DIEPEN	Scheeps. Gebr. van Diepen N.V., Groningen, Holland
VAN DUIVENDIJK	N. V. van Duivendijk, Holland
WAAL	De Waal Scheeps. N. V., Havendijk, Holland
WESER	A.G. Weser, Bremerhaven.
WHITE	J. Samuel White & Co. Ltd, Cowes
WILLIAMSON	R. Williamson & Son Ltd, Workington
YARWOOD	W. J. Yarwood & Sons Ltd, Northwich